CEREAL
DAD PRENEUR

Put Your Family First
While You Build An Empire And Create Wealth

MATT SMITH

You have to read Cereal Dad Preneur!
I am neither a Dad nor an entrepreneur but the info in this book is for anyone wanting to advance in life. It benefited me and helped guide me to better my life choices in more ways than one. From improving mindset and work ethic to enjoying family life even more. 100% recommend this book to everyone.
~ Isaiah Gonzales

This book is a great source of inspiration that will tell the story of what it takes to become a successful entrepreneur and family man.
~ Leann Vezanni

Everyone wants to know how Matt Smith does it. He reveals all of his secrets in this book to win. It's a must read for any person that has a passion for life.
~ Jenny

If you want t o understand the importance of succeeding in BUSINESS and, more importantly, in LIFE, read this book!!!!
~ Chris Turner

Matt packages his own guide to help both men and women reach for more in business, balance and life, but written from the perspective of a friend.
~ Adam Sanchez

CEREAL DAD PRENEUR
Put Your Family First
While You Build An Empire And Create Wealth

Copyright @ 2021 Matt Smith

First published 2021 Christine Robinson Global

ISBN: Amazon Print 9798594723504

All rights reserved. Without limiting the rights under copyright reserved above, no part of this publication may be reproduced, stored in or introduced into a database and retrieval system or transmitted in any form or any means (electronic, mechanical, photocopying, recording or otherwise) without the prior written permission of both the owner of copyright and the publishers.

The people, events and information contained within this Book are strictly for educational purposes. If you wish to apply ideas contained in this Book, you are taking full responsibility for your actions. This publication is designed to provide accurate and authoritative information regarding the subject matter covered. It is sold with the understanding that the author and the publisher are not engaged in rendering legal, accounting, or other professional services. If you require legal advice or other expert assistance, you should seek the services of a competent professional.

Disclaimer: The author makes no guarantees to the results you'll achieve by reading this book. All business requires risk and hard work. The results and client case studies presented in this book represent results achieved working directly with the author. Your results may vary when undertaking any new business venture or marketing strategy.

Throughout the book I have gifts to help propel you further, faster.

Open the link below to access your Book Bonus gifts
https://cerealdadpreneur.com/bookbonuses

You can find Matt here:

📘 https://www.facebook.com/mattsmithcerealdadpreneur

📷 https://www.instagram.com/mattsmithpueblo

✉️ matt@cerealdadpreneur.com

🌐 www.wakeuppueblo.com

FOREWORD
by Grant Cardone

Cereal Dad Preneur is a MUST read. For anyone trying to do it all in business and not having to compromise your role as a parent and spouse, you have to read this book. Matt Smith is seriously a unique and profound individual who has miraculously codified how to balance life, as best as a person can.

If you are one of those people who want to build a business, and pursue your dreams, all while being a great partner, parent, and still fulfill all of your other demands and responsibilities, you know how hard it is. Matt is one of those very special people, few of whom I have met in my 40 years traveling the world, who doesn't talk about how it should be; he loves it and he lives it, and he was generous enough to share his secrets with you.

First meet Matt in this great read and you will adopt his infectious, positive attitude and outlook on life. You're going to feel the stress of life become less jaded and have a plan to be the best YOU at everything you do, just like Matt.

Want to figure out how to get it all done; grow your business, make quality time for family, charity, community, employees, and still take care of your personal development and health *Cereal Dad Preneur* will show you how.

Table of Contents

Introduction 11

Lesson 1
The Power of WHY 16

LESSON 2
Positivity is a Muscle 37

LESSON 3
BENDing Time 52

LESSON 4
Two Ears, One Mouth
  - Art Of Communication 92

LESSON 5
Be the Best You
  - Strong Body, Strong Mind, Strong Heart 105

LESSON 6
Adapt and Transform 125

LESSON 7
Who's on your Bus? Culture, Systems, And People ... 142

LESSON 8
Growth 164

LESSON 9
Integrity and Gratitude 183

LESSON 10
Memories 199

Final Words 218

This book took me years to write. As you read it, you will notice that some of the stories and examples were definitely from the time before COVID-19 triggered a global health crisis. The massive shutdown completely altered our daily schedules and our very way of life. This interruption in my typical routine created, among other things, the window of time for me to finish writing this book.

This was also a crazy and exciting time, as for almost two months of the writing process I was also being followed virtually 24/7 by a large Discovery Channel TV crew for the filming of "Undercover Billionaire!!"

Wow what an amazing ride :) You can find out more about 'behind the scenes' of the show and my meeting Grant Cardone and our growing relationship very soon, as I have two more books in production.

Dedication

Thanks to my amazing wife Jenny, son Parker, daughter Paisley, and son Preston. You are the reason that I continue to try harder and continue to grow to be a better person. You are my WHY and why I am so committed to Family First.

Thanks to my angel above my mother who still inspires me daily in life and death to be the person I am today. And thanks to my amazing family for all the support and motivation you have ever given me.

To anyone who I have crossed your path or you have crossed mine. Thanks for your inspiration and motivation to make me into who I am today. I would not be who I am today without the love of my hometown Pueblo, Colorado and the amazing people who are in it.

For making my dream into a reality with writing a book, thank you Christine Robinson (Empress On Fire) for all your hard work and dedication to this project. You are the best in the industry and I am lucky to have you throughout this process. You have now become such an inspiration in my life and friend through this. Also, thanks to Judy Halish who edited my horrible grammar and helped tell my story with her wordcraft, I can't thank you enough.

Thanks Wake Up Pueblo for the art and book cover.

Picture Paige Shemenauer

Cover Jacob Rivera & Christine Robinson

Introduction

"Twenty years from now you will be more disappointed by the things that you didn't do than by the ones you did. So throw off the bowlines. Sail away from the safe harbor. Catch the trade winds in your sails. Explore. Dream. Discover."

~ Mark Twain

Being an entrepreneur was in my blood from an early age. I started my adventure in the business world in grade school, selling gum out of my locker, mowing lawns, and running paper routes to make money. Today, I consider myself a "Serial Entrepreneur". I have created and developed at least ten different businesses, all of which continue to grow and thrive in my amazing but small hometown of Pueblo, Colorado. The most surprising thing about my endeavors is they are each in different industries. Since I was not an expert in any of them, the key to my success was developing systems that worked across diverse industries.

While I am proud that I've busted my butt and earned everything I have, I'm also grateful and blessed beyond belief. Writing this book has challenged me at many levels, but sharing my stories and writing about what I've achieved in my life, tested me more than I expected. My coaches kept reminding me that telling my stories isn't about bragging; it's about helping you see that I have the expertise and proven success to help you achieve your dream.

People often ask me, "What motivates you?" My wife, Jenny, and my three children, Parker, Paisley, and Preston, are my driving force and my "BIG WHY". Growing up as the son of a single mom, I had the opportunity to see the struggles and triumphs of putting family first while working full-time. My mom, Kathy Jean Luke, was amazing and taught me that parenting is the most loving journey you will ever take. She may not have had a lot of money, but what my mom lacked in funds, she more than made up for in love for her family.

I cherish those early memories, and the lessons are woven into the fabric of my being. Now, as a "Dad-preneur", I strive to be the best family man, best entrepreneur and the healthiest person I can be. That's not always easy! I am sure many of you struggle with these same challenges.

Some of you are rocking the "Dad" part of your life! You are always at your kid's soccer or baseball games, helping with homework, capitalizing on life's teachable moments because you are present and participating. However, your vision for that radical idea or revolutionary business is on the back burner, waiting until you have more time, when your kids are older. In the meantime, you languish

Introduction

at a mediocre unfulfilling job that does not feed your soul. Does this sound like you?

How many of you are the opposite? You're a rock star in the business arena, at the top of your game in the office, respected and admired by co-workers. You focus all of your energy developing your empire or climbing the corporate ladder. But your relationships pay the price. You have not been present with your family to participate in their lives, to be a strong role model for them, or to watch them grow. Have you missed birthdays, anniversaries, your baby's first steps or first words, your son's first hit in baseball, your daughter's first robotics competition or dance recital? If that's you, then neither you nor your family have many memories of sharing those special times with you. Is this really the life you intended to create? Is this really the measure of your success?

Or are you someone who is stuck right in the middle, never feeling like you excel in either aspect of your life? Grinding on the treadmill day in and day out working long hours, yet never really winning. Maybe you are in a middle management job with little prospects of growth; your hopes are fading into distant memories and eroding your self-confidence, leaving you feeling like you have less to offer to your family. Both your relationships and your business are stagnant.

My intent with "Life Lessons from a Serial Dadpreneur" is to present you a road map and a practical guide to achieve success in all areas of your life. I sincerely appreciate your picking up this book and taking the time to read it. I hope you take away a couple of golden nuggets such as how to build exceptional systems, boost your communication, manage your time, get your positive on, and take control of your health, to name a few.

While I speak from the perspective of a dad because that's who I am, I also acknowledge there are plenty of amazing "Mom-preneurs" out there who face similar or even greater challenges. These universal themes will help you too. FAMILY FIRST has always been my motto, but that doesn't have to come at the expense of pursuing your ambitions and passions of being wildly successful in business at the same time. You CAN have it all and feel good about yourself and your achievements.

I'm not perfect, but I continue to grow and improve every day. Everyone is on a journey, and I want to save the "Dad-preneur" in you a massive amount of time and effort. What if I could propel you along the learning curve to a place light-years ahead of where you are now, by helping you benefit from my life experiences while bypassing some of my challenges? When you study these lessons and implement the tools and techniques provided, you will develop the systems you need to succeed in any industry, allowing you to work smarter. I promise it will change your life for the better.

I have total financial freedom, am married to the love of my life, and blessed with three amazing, respectful, healthy children. I live in my dream home, with a second home in the mountains. I am healthy and have traveled the world. I can honestly say I am **living my best life every day** and loving every minute of it. None of this is by coincidence. It's all by design because I refuse to settle for anything less than this life. I worked my ass off, growing my aspirations into reality. You can achieve your best life by applying what I have learned and putting in place the right strategies and systems.

Don't let another day go by without taking action to grab hold of the balanced life you and your family deserve. Accelerate your journey to success. Let me teach you the secrets that allowed me to retire in my 30's. Open your mind, roll up your sleeves, and get to work on you!

Lesson 1

The Power of WHY

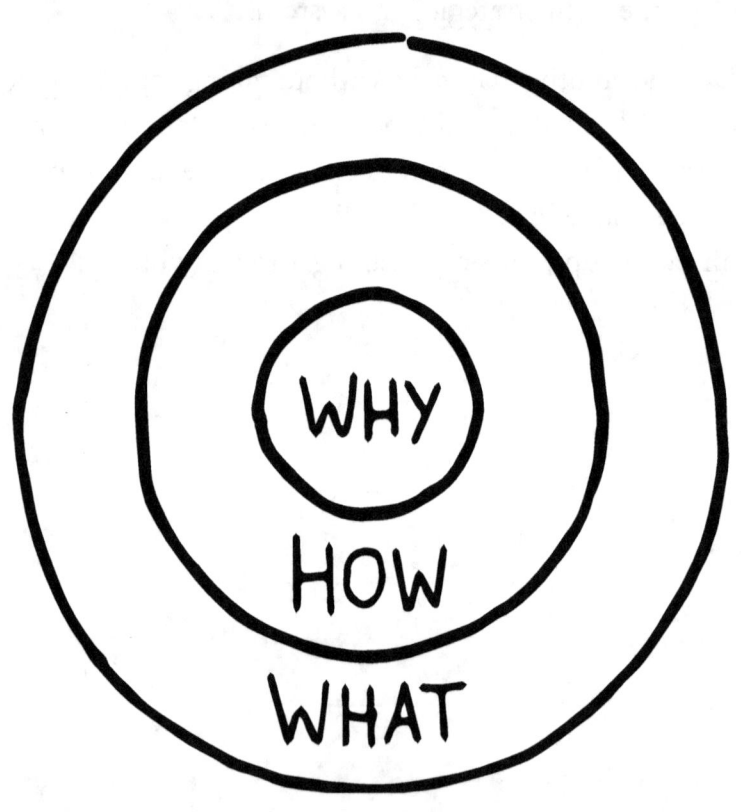

The Power of WHY

Finding your why is the most important thing you could ever do for yourself. When you wake up in the morning, do you know what inspires you? What drives you? What is your purpose? Knowing your Why is key to living our best life.

When we begin anything new, a habit, routine, program, mindset, or way of life, we all want to jump right into the HOW, but it's paramount first to ask yourself, "WHY?" Take a moment now and consider these questions:

Why am I doing this?

Why now?

Why make this particular change?

Why haven't I done this before?

Why do I think it will be different this time?

If your answer is because you want to be wealthy, what does that truly mean to you? If your answer is that you want to be the best dad, what does it look like to you? Put your dream into specific terms. Most of us can immediately come up with some intangible ideal to answer these questions about the life we desire. The problem with an idea is you don't genuinely have a clear picture of what that translates to in concrete terms. If you can't imagine how this vision manifests in your everyday life, it will never come to fruition. You need to dig beyond the first answer that comes to mind. Fully embrace within your body, mind, and spirit what you desire. You must be able to see and feel it with certainty, and the most critical component to a powerful Why is that you must believe you can achieve what you desire. Explore your driving force. Later in this chapter, there's an exercise to help you determine your WHY and to see if your WHY, will stand up to the test of time, challenges, and obstacles. You might be asking why the Why is so important? Good question!

Have you ever noticed how many people are 100 percent committed to a new fitness regime on a Monday? I've been in the gym business for 13 years, and I can tell you first-hand, gyms are typically packed on Mondays, especially Mondays in January, after they have just made a New Year's resolution to "get healthy." But where are they by Wednesday or Thursday or in February or March? Month after month and year after year, I see the same pattern. Almost 80% of people do not succeed in making significant lifestyle changes. People want to make the change; they fail because their WHY is not strong enough to carry them through challenging times.

Knowing your WHY comes into play here. If you are very clear about WHY you want to make a particular change, then when you run into the inevitable obstacles or excuses like:

- It's too hard
- It takes too much time
- I'm not good at that yet
- I would rather sleep in
- I would rather hang out with my friends
- I'll just take the short-cut this one time
- It's not working yet
- It didn't work for me last time I tried
- It didn't work for my friend, Steve
- I'll start tomorrow
- Next week is MY week

You can remind yourself WHY you started this in the first place and WHY you are trying to change your life for the better. A crystal clear Why fuels rock-solid motivation and conviction. Knowing and believing whole-heartedly in your WHY is key to your success at the HOW.

YOUR TIME IS NOW!!

My WHY is my family: I have always been a FAMILY FIRST kind of guy. I learned this vital lesson from my loving mother who never failed to make our family the most important aspect of her life. In the same way, my wife and kids are the center of my world. What exactly does Family First mean? For me, it means that I will do everything in my power to protect my family. It also means that I am willing to lose it all for them. It means I will work my ass off to succeed in business so my family can have the best life possible, and every opportunity they deserve. I want my legacy to be more than just a successful businessman. I want to be known as a "Serial Entrepreneur," who lived for his family, loved the thrill of business and entrepreneurship, and did all he could to give back to his community. Without your family, your money is worthless. So if you are struggling at home but good at work or struggling at work but good at home, keep reading because I am obsessed with success and making my stamp in the business world. Yet, I am even more committed to ensuring that my kids grow up to be remarkable humans. I will not accept anything less than that! Now, I want to help you make your mark as a successful dad and entrepreneur.

I can remember distinctly, the very moment this all became crystal clear to me. I was 18 years old and lying in a hospital bed. We didn't have a lot when I was growing up. My mom was working full-time and raising two young boys on her own. She was unbelievably generous. I remember watching her give a homeless person the last dollar in her wallet, and then a few days later, our electricity was turned off because she hadn't paid that bill. She would say to my brother and me, "It's okay, I get paid in a few days, and we have a roof over our heads." She always had faith that God would take care of us, and we would be okay. She found her abundance in loving and caring for us and giving back to her community. She used to take us on day trips up to the mountains near

Lake Isabel. We would go hiking and skip rocks on the lake. The stories she would tell us about 'Bishops Castle' left an impression on me about what can be achieved when you are determined and follow your dreams. My mom was so proud of my brother and me that she couldn't wait to have us meet her patients at the nursing home. Sometimes we would sing to the patients or bring our rabbits for them to pet. To us, at the time, these were little things. It wasn't until I became a father that I truly understood what it meant for my mother to bring us to work and "show us off", how as a parent that can fill your heart. I also gained a whole other level of appreciation for her when I learned how much work, dedication, and love it takes to raise children, and I don't have to do it as a single parent the way she did. She just loved being a mom so much. We were her big WHY. She taught us right from wrong, how to be decent people, and how little things that don't cost much can mean everything. Through the example of her life, we learned how to live a life of passion and purpose.

Every town has its "rough" section, which people usually avoid, especially at night. Back then, in Pueblo, that's the east side. When you live or go to school in this part of town, you learn to navigate it. You develop mutual respect and tolerance for people regardless of race, socio-economic background, or gang affiliation.

In High School, I was in the Reserve Officers' Training Corps (ROTC) and choir, but I struggled academically. The difficulty was not due to a lack of effort; it stemmed from so many ideas bouncing around my head that I couldn't focus or retain information. Most of my friends at East Pueblo High were athletic students. We took school seriously and loved to play sports and hang out together. We were, and still are a pretty tight bunch and always had each other's backs. Like most guys our age, we enjoyed socializing at house parties or local bars. I was never known as a fighter, I was more the peacemaker in our group. We always looked out for each other, so if trouble started, I had their back.

New Year's Eve 1999, I went with a group of my closest friends to an epic party on the east side at a friend's house. The house was packed, people upstairs and downstairs inside the house. There was even a crowd on the deck off the back of the house. The party was so big that the groups spilled out into the adjacent grocery store's parking lot. The music was pumping, beer flowing, everyone having a great time celebrating ushering in the New Year.

One of my friends was having some trouble with another guy, so I tried to diffuse the situation and prevent a fight. I told him we were all there to have a good time and enjoy the party. I thought it would blow over and went back to the party. Hours later, out of nowhere 25, or 30 gang members showed up, and everything changed. I felt like we were instantly plunged into one of those great battle scenes from a movie.

Picture the scene: It's a dark night, a couple of hundred spectators between the deck, yard and parking lot, and two groups of guys in a standoff. Me and my buddies, eight athletic college-age guys, merely wanting to have a good time at a party on one side. Across from us, there was a group of 25 or 30 gang members. While the gang members were smaller guys, they had broomsticks, baseball bats, tire irons, and knives. They didn't come to the party to celebrate; they came for only one reason – a brutal fight!

Time slowed to that speed where you can feel yourself falling but can't stop it. I stood there for a moment; it felt like an eternity. My heart was pounding, my eyes blinking in disbelief. I thought, "This isn't really going to happen, is it?" Everyone at the party was now glued to this movie scene about to play out in front of them. I couldn't believe no one was going to intervene and try to stop this from happening.

Just then, someone yelled something, and a broomstick came flying at us out of the darkness. Then BOOM, in a flash, chaos erupted. In a split second, the two groups were on top of each other, and everything became a blur. There was a moment that I remember pulling guys off of my friends. I was trying to fight as many of them as I could at once. Suddenly, there was this searing hot sensation in my back, but the adrenaline was coursing through my body, and the battle raged on so I couldn't even feel the pain. When the dust settled, someone in the audience yelled, "Oh God, you're bleeding!" I reached around to discover my back soaked in blood.

As jaw-dropping as all that sounds, the pivotal moment was still to come.

I spent a couple of days in the hospital where I found out that the laceration was only an inch away from my spine, and I could easily have been paralyzed or killed. I remember my mom, the nurse sitting there comforting me. At the same time, she was scared out of her mind because she fully understood the severity of the situation and how close I came to death or permanent injury. She was so supportive and not judgmental of me. Other parents might have scolded their son in this situation, trying to get him to recognize the potential consequences of his actions. Not my mom, outwardly, Mom never wavered from her encouragement and loving affirmation that we would get through this, and everything would be okay. Internally, she wrestled with what any good parent would be asking, "How can I better protect my son?" She talked about sending me to a military school or even to Texas to live with my father, who at the time, I hardly knew.

That's when it happened. Lying there in the hospital bed, I saw my grandmother, my mother's mother. She walked up to the door of my room, never saying a word, she just stood there, shook her head in disbelief, a look of disgust on her face. She turned around and walked out without even coming in to see me. I saw her face, and I felt this tremendous guilt. The pit of my stomach seized, and I looked at my mom. I thought about all that she had done for me and realized the heartache that I was causing her. That's when reality hit me that I was the one responsible for my mother's grief!

At that moment, something snapped, and all at once I saw my life play out before me; what I was doing, my poor decisions, where that would take me, and who I would become if I didn't change. I thought to myself, Who the hell am I? Why am I doing this? I know I am better than this! Right then and there, I decided, this wasn't the path for my life, and I was going to do whatever it took to change.

Oddly enough, lying there in that hospital bed, seeing my grandmother's raw emotions, was the best thing ever. That was my pivotal moment, my turning point. I grew up. I stopped going to parties and bars every single night with my friends, and I never fought again.

In my quest to improve my life, I shifted my approach from working any job I could for the paycheck to finding a career with growth potential. Before my pivotal moment, I had several jobs, often two at a time, ranging from prep dishwasher and telemarketing to phone sales. I even worked at Discount Tire, which was both physically demanding and a fantastic customer service experience. With each position, I added a new skill to my growing professional tool belt.

After that New Year's Eve, I took a position selling Cell Phones from a booth in Walmart. One day, I caught the eye of a representative from the Denver Mattress Company. Adam Graham was a mentor of mine growing up and the son of my mom's best friend. He saw my potential and recruited me for a job in the sales department at the Denver Mattress Company. I was grateful that all the effort I had put into becoming a better me, paid off. I pushed myself to learn quickly and became the top salesperson. Within the first year, while I was still only 19 years old, I was promoted to Assistant Manager of the Colorado Springs store.

During my 18 years with Denver Mattress, I was fortunate to have one of the most amazing mentors, Darrell Bain. He was and continues to be one of the most influential men in my life. He taught me to love the sales process, be a person of integrity, and earn rather than demand the respect of my team members. Within two years, at age 21, I was the manager of the Pueblo store. During this time, I found a way to start investing in real estate and set my sights on building a life both my mother and grandmother would be proud of, and I have never looked back.

I attempted college four or five times at Colorado State University (CSU) Pueblo, and although I tried very hard, I dropped out each time. I discovered that I had trouble with reading retention. I could read the same book eight times and not know what I had just read. Then when it came to the tests, I could never remember anything because I had not fully understood what I was reading. Eventually, the doctor's diagnosed me with ADD and ADHD. Now that I have learned how to leverage my condition and harness all that energy in my brain differently, I see it as a blessing, and I am successful at the things I tackle. The funny thing is CSU Pueblo invited me to participate in their version of "Shark Tank." I am now a regular judge and investor in their program, even though I never graduated from college. Don't think I'm anti-college; I learned a lot in college. At the time, I couldn't figure out how to make it work for me. If it's your path, figure out how to make it work for you, and if you need help along the way, ask until you succeed. Even if you don't complete a degree program, you can still achieve your goals in your way.

When college did not work out for me, I knew there had to be a different way to build my future beyond my job at the mattress store. I had dreams, and I was determined to make them a reality. A good friend's mother was a realtor. I was fascinated by that world, so she helped me figure out how to buy my first personal residence and then a rental property. Once I successfully did that, I had an "aha moment" and thought, "that wasn't as hard as I thought it was going to be. I can do this!" I bought several more rentals and got into fixing and flipping houses.

My newfound success at both the mattress company and in the world of real estate had me earning more money than I ever saw growing up. So like most people, feeling flush for the first time, I splurged on a big weekend. I took a friend to New Orleans and spent what I considered a lot of money. By Monday morning, I decided, the $500 could do so much more for my future if I had spent it more wisely.

After that realization, I shifted my mindset. Don't get me wrong, I still spent money having fun with friends, but I was much more conscious of my financial decisions. More often, I spent my money on business lunches where I could acquire valuable knowledge from an industry leader or mentor about business, real estate, or life. I asked a lot of questions, and those meetings paid significant returns on my investments. Knowing your objective will help prepare you for these types of meetings. Leveraging local talent is an incredibly valuable tool. Find people who are smarter than you or are further along the path you want to travel. Become part of their circle. Get a glimpse inside the mind of a subject matter expert. I was surprised at how willing people were to tell their story, share their experiences and help.

I was amazed at how much knowledge I gained between those meetings and audio books. Everything I learned along the way reminded me to stay laser-focused on my why. I started implementing those powerful lessons. One of the books I read was "Rich Dad, Poor Dad" by Robert Kiyosaki. From that point on, as I was making money, I saved every dime or made it work for me. I learned to save and leverage my money so well that even in the worst economic time in my life 2008, when the US real estate market crashed, I opened my first business, a Snap Fitness franchise. Over the next few years, I built it into the largest location in the country. The philosophies and strategies I learned in those early days were priceless and continue to guide me today.

Based on what I learned in real estate, I found a process that worked for me and I created systems that allowed me to duplicate the results. I felt free to try my hand at businesses in any industry because I now had a winning formula. This confidence started my path as a "Serial-Entrepreneur".

The Party Bus business was kind of a fluke. After I won it on eBay, I realized everyone wanted it, and a light bulb went on. "Maybe I should rent it out and make some money?" So even though I bought it for fun, I seized the moment and turned it into a business. I expanded it by adding several other buses before selling the business. It was pretty ironic because I wasn't as focused on partying, but I had a knack for putting them together.

> As it turns out, the party bus was a safer and more cost-effective way to have fun with my friends!

About this time, I was trying to schedule a carpet cleaning. All the local carpet cleaners were booked for more than two weeks in advance. Of course, I saw it as an opportunity. If everyone is so busy, it must mean that this is a service that is in high demand. Without hesitation, I bought the equipment, a used van, hired a team, and started my carpet cleaning business. Never in a million years did I think I would ever get into the carpet cleaning business, but when I spot an opening or hole in the market, I have to jump on it.

Another example of how I identify opportunities and quickly take action; I met Tawnya Gibbs, one of the best massage therapists in the area, and learned what it takes to be profitable in the spa industry. Together, we identified suitable space in my existing fitness building, hired staff, and opened the spa. We took her one-room operation and turned it into the largest spa in southern Colorado. Eventually, I sold her the business, helping create another entrepreneur.

My ongoing real estate experience was a huge asset when I decided to look for commercial property to purchase. After paying someone else's commercial mortgage for six years, my lease was scheduled to renew for another five years. I learned that I could build a 10,000 square foot building for a little more than I was paying to lease the 3,000 square foot space. The math seemed like a no-brainer! So I built my own Snap Fitness building. Five years later, I expanded from the 10,000 square foot building to a 30,000 square foot building without spending any of my money. Instead, I leveraged the equity in the first gym to build the second and leased six commercial spaces housing complimentary services, to help pay my new LARGE mortgage.

One of the ways my ADD ADHD helps me is to see the many opportunities that most other people would overlook. Instead of being overwhelmed, I channel my brain energy toward these many projects. After completing the building for Snap Fitness, the building next door became available, and well once again an opportunity knocked and BOOM I jumped. This is my new mattress company, Snooze Mattress Co.

In all that I've learned, the experts will all tell you to live within your means. My additional advice is to apply these concepts to both your business and personal life and be sure to stay aligned with your why. There's always a hard way and a smart way to grow. Living within your means is the smart way to grow. Each time I upgrade my primary residence, I apply all the profits from the current house to the down payment for the new house, thereby leveling up rather than incurring more debt. That way, the mortgage stays the same even though we have a larger or more beautiful home in a great location. Three houses later, we are living in our dream house with basically the same mortgage payment as the first house. Every time I walk around my home, I have to pinch myself, knowing how blessed we are. I am proud that I used the same level up strategy for my home as I did with my businesses

> **Don't let anyone tell you that you can't accomplish something. If I can, so can you!**

when I constructed larger buildings and didn't incur additional debt.

So why do I share my story with you? I want you to know that you can turn around any situation from your past or present and start fresh immediately. It's the clarity and strength of your Why that will help you. Today can be your DAY 1. Life doesn't care if you're lying in a hospital bed, sitting in jail, getting divorced, or headed for homelessness. You can create a "Do-Over." While you can continue to reboot yourself over and over, make this time count. Use this re-start to refine and redefine the 'You' you want to be, and recommit to your 'Why.' There are no false starts, only beginnings that haven't worked yet. Keep getting up, and do it as many times as you need, because one of these versions will stick. My greatest desire for you is that with my help through this book, this is the time that will click and move you forward to a new life.

Start now, and you can turn your current situation into your best life!

I didn't have much money growing up, nor was anything ever handed to me. I didn't have it easy. I had to make bold choices and then follow through with my actions to change my path. Just like me, you can choose that today is the day you shift your thoughts about what you're worth and deserve. Identify your 'why,' take action and reap the reward of success.

I identified my BIG WHY, asked for help, dug deep, was knocked down and got back up over and over again. Getting knocked down comes with the territory.

I know that you can do this! DON'T STOP! You'll come up against obstacles along the way; the key is to find a way to run right through or around any obstacle. When you keep trying and don't give up is when the magic happens. Believe me, whatever situation you're trying to improve, it will, you just have to have faith, a plan, and grit. This book is an inside look at what I do and provides you with a way to make necessary changes in your life to achieve your dreams.

This exercise will help you define your own WHY. Complete this before you begin the Lessons in this book.

Defining and Aligning Your Goals

First, think about what your "best life" looks like in all aspects of your life. Either write or draw it out or dictate it into your phone. Describe in detail everything you see, think, and feel in this ideal life.

- Where do you live?
- How is your health?
- What does the average day look like?
- How happy is your family?
- How solid are your relationships?
- Where does your income come from?

- How many hours are you spending with family and friends?
- How many hours do you spend on you?
- How many hours are you spending at work?
- How are you growing personally and professionally?
- What ways do you give back to your community, family, and business?

Next, take a hard look at your current life. How does it compare with your dream life? What areas need the most improvement? Where do you want to start making changes?

Now you know:

- your reason for wanting to grow and make significant changes (**WHY**) and
- you have a clear picture of what your goal is (**WHAT**)

The best way to use this book to learn the 'HOW' is to start with the lesson that resonates most with you. It might be the area that needs the most work or the one that feels the most comfortable to focus on first. You choose.

As you start to work on one aspect of your life, you will also notice things begin to improve in other areas of your life. The strategies taught in these lessons apply to both your family life and your business life. In this balancing act between family and business, mastering a series of core skills and learning to use them in both hemispheres will strengthen your proficiency. This approach will also save you time since you don't have to learn a completely different set of tools for managing each part of your life. Eventually, you will want to visit each lesson to pick up a nugget or two to help round out your growth process in all areas. Achieving balance is not the same as striving for perfection.

Frequently revisit the "Defining and Aligning Your Goals" exercise to see your progress. The Why that you define must become an integral part of your day-to-day life, so review it daily. This simple action directs your mind to focus on activities and thoughts that will strengthen your commitment. This exercise will feed your momentum and enable you to make necessary course corrections along the way to ensure that you keep your big picture in mind. This step isn't something you do once and forget about it. It's not a Monday in January at the gym where you get credit for just showing up. It's a life-changing event to create a better you as a parent, business person, and human.

You picked up this book for a reason; you must want to improve some aspect of your life. You deserve it. Give 100% and persevere until you succeed. Use this exercise and these lessons to win now and in the future!

Key Lesson Takeaways

- ✓ Get crystal clear clarity on your big WHY
- ✓ Create a visual aid that depicts your why (images/words)
- ✓ Review your Why Daily
- ✓ Identify mentors and coaches to help clarify your WHY
- ✓ Anticipate your obstacles
- ✓ Develop a resource list and strategy to overcome obstacles

Jenny's Advice

My WHY is to have a happy and healthy family, have faith, and try to make a difference in as many lives as possible in the time we have. Don't let life pass you by! We get to be the author of our own life story, so why not make it the best book we've ever read?

LESSON 2
Positivity is a Muscle

> *"We can spend time training for work, training at the gym, but when was the last time you trained your attitude?"*
>
> ~ Matt Smith

Most people see positivity as a mindset. I see it as a muscle that you need to train every day. Just like in the weight room, where one workout by itself does not build enormous biceps, the positivity muscle is something you need to sculpt daily. You should work it, strengthen it, and throw challenges at it until it can withstand anything. Positivity will permeate all aspects of your life once you embrace it as a default attitude. It took me a while and a lot of repetition to get to where I am now, but it's entirely worth it. One thing that always works for me to feed my positivity is to get up early and start my day with a cardio workout while listening to an audiobook to stimulate my brain. I choose my attitude; it doesn't control me. Positivity is a choice. When you are so consistently positive that it prompts people to ask, "Do you ever have a bad day?" then you know you have conquered negativity. It's not even in your vocabulary.

When you first begin focusing on positivity, you might discover that just like muscles, you'll need to practice because it's easy to slide back into negativity and not even realize until it's pointed out to you. Grow positivity within your world through your words, actions, and feelings. Share the importance of positivity with your employees and family. You have probably heard that like minds think alike. Well, that is undoubtedly true about positivity. Have you ever noticed that negative people attract other negative people? To limit your exposure to negativity, implement a news-fast, or at least monitor your news viewing and how you feel during and after watching. Observing yourself is an excellent way to gauge its effects on you and your reactions. Likewise, positive people are magnets for other positive people. If everyone around you is practicing positivity, looking for ways to express positive words, thoughts, and feelings, you'll soon surround yourself with employees, family, and a community of positive people.

COVID 19, causing the global pandemic of 2020, provided a perfect opportunity to practice positivity. Without a doubt, an epic medical crisis of this proportion is cause for concern. It requires us to pay attention to the guidance of medical experts worldwide to know what we need to do to be as safe as reasonably possible. Some people allow themselves to be consumed by the fear, panic, and uncertainty of the situation while others can stay informed without becoming paralyzed by the negativity. While it is tragic that so many lives are being lost or upended, I decided from the beginning that something good was going to come out of this for me, my family, and my work teams.

Like other positive people, I found ways to work within the constraints imposed to contain the virus by shifting the way I view this time. I look at it as a gift. Never before have so many people, except essential workers, had so much time at home. Instead of feeling powerless and trapped, I view this time with my family and the creative way my teams are connecting through technology as an opportunity to grow deeper bonds, improve our approach to customer service, strengthen our communication and enrich ourselves personally and professionally. In the Lesson on Growth, I share many of the innovative ideas we used during this time. It has forced me to re-evaluate how I do everything and given me the time to create new habits that change my blueprint.

When it comes to positivity, I choose to walk the walk and look for ways to express and expand positivity. Therefore, I decided to keep my employees on the payroll rather than laying off or downsizing. I have faith that we will come through this stronger, but only if we do it together. Paying my employees was not a handout, rather a way to show how much I value and believe in them. My teams did not have to worry about filing for unemployment, paying bills, or feeding their families. I feel for those around the world who are at this time, concerned for personal safety and security. I believe that my ability to continue to pay my employees has provided them a feeling of safety. This security is one way to create a positive experience and demonstrates my appreciation for all of their hard work.

Think about how much more you get done when you are in a positive mindset than a negative one. Things are in flow when you are coming from a place of positivity. You direct your energy productively and efficiently. Positivity is a healthy state of being, and the strongest positive emotion is love.

Love is a choice, so choose love. Show it with your words and your actions. Love everyone that comes onto your path. An interesting thing about love is that sometimes those individuals most in need of love will resist receiving it. Try not to judge others; just send out a prayer or positive thought to spread love to everyone.

When we genuinely care about other people, we express an interest in them and their families. We listen and offer support and encouragement to others. This caring is a form of love. I have learned that people don't care what you know until they know how much you care. When people realize that you've taken time from your day to care about them, they become more receptive and open to you. Each time you have an exchange based on caring and love, you create a positive momentum and ripple effect through all your relationships.

As a parent, it is your job to stay positive for your kids and think about their foundation and their future. The skills and mindsets you teach them at an early age will be the groundwork for building their dreams and reality. Too often, parents do not realize or pay attention to the effect they have on their children. We have all seen or heard too many examples. You have heard a parent say, "my kid is not an athlete; he reads books" right in front of their child. What do you think that tells him? How do you think he internalizes that statement? He hears, "You suck at sports and should never play them." Or, the parent says, "My kid is shy." What do you think that tells a kid growing up? There is a good chance these kids will grow up shy and not playing sports because of what they have consistently heard from a young age. If you continue to tell him he is not good at sports or is shy, your child assumes that they are flawed or deficient in some way, and most kids will withdraw further.

Instead, what if you're more positive when talking to and about your child? You could say, "he is getting better every day at sports, and if he keeps putting his heart into it, he will be amazing." Alternatively, try, "Give him a minute: he's just warming up to you." When you make an effort to turn your statements into positive and encouraging remarks, they will have profoundly positive effects on your child. You teach them that it's okay to try something that they are reluctant or scared to do. It's okay if they are not exceptional right out of the gate. A little positive reinforcement is incredibly powerful. It goes a long way in the healthy development of a child. Feed your children a steady diet of positivity.

Positivity is a Muscle

When my oldest son Parker was five years old, someone told him he was getting chubby. Realistically, my son was nowhere near chubby, but his younger sister was petite by comparison. I could tell he was playing tough until I asked him about it, he confessed he thought maybe it was right and it deeply affected him. I could have told him it was nonsense and blown it off, but instead, I decided to take this on as a personal challenge to help him get through. Every day we would go on hikes or do small workouts together, and I told him how buff he was getting. Within weeks he stopped feeling bad about that remark, and I never heard him say that he was chubby again. Instead, he now flexes his muscles and shows us how buff he is. Imagine what could have happened if I had let that go if I had let him continue thinking he was chubby. If I didn't take the time to be a positive influence and give him the tools to change how he feels about himself, he could have grown up believing in an offhand comment. I say, "Take a hammer to that kind of BS and move on!"

Here's another way as a Dad, I teach positivity to my kids. I use a great tip that I learned from my good friend and someone I admire, George Carroll. Every morning when I drive my kids to school, I ask them, "Is today going to be a great day?" **They will scream at me with genuine excitement, "Yes, because we're gonna make it a great day!"**

You can call it brainwashing or whatever you want, but kids learn to believe what you believe and what they see. By starting every day this way, I help them get excited about life and understand that they have a choice about how they see the world and experience their day. This is huge. I am so passionate about positivity that I'm writing a children's book called "Today's Going to Be A Great Day" to help parents teach positivity to their children at an early age. I also frequently tell my kids that they are each other's best friends, and they need to protect and look out for one another, no matter what.

My wife, Jenny, and I believe in treating our children as adults in the sense that if they do something wrong instead of scolding them or smacking them, we sit them down and talk with them. We hear them out, listening for how they were feeling and what they thought in the decision they made. Then we calmly explain our concerns and why we might feel it was a wrong decision. Giving them a chance to tell their side and also to understand our viewpoint helps them to grasp the bigger picture and sets the proper expectation for similar situations in the future.

The same rules of positivity apply at work. As the manager, owner, even co-worker, you should be positive with the people around you and over-communicate. Become the type of manager who attracts people through their positivity. Do this, and everyone will want to work for you! When you create a culture based on positivity, fun, personal accountability, and honesty, it will also foster open communication, and people will enjoy being at work.

As a manager, you can never know how much of an impact your positive interactions with your employees are making until they are tested. My business teams know that everything I do benefits everyone. Recently, a competitor approached one of my managers and attempted to recruit him for their store. As he relayed the story to me, he said to them, ""Even if it's a little more money in the short term, why would I ever leave Matt?" The competitor said, "Matt, will leave you behind as he builds his empire." My manager's reply was, "That's not true, Matt shares his vision for the company, so I know we are all part of his big picture!" This incredible manager knows me well enough to know I want my co-workers to stick around because I think the journey will be awesome because we're together! I value and respect my employees like family. The associate was so confident in my relationship with my employees, he not only turned down the offer but also felt comfortable telling me about the exchange.

One of your primary roles as a leader in the business is to communicate clear expectations and teach your co-workers how to do things within the company. How you go about imparting those lessons will directly influence how well the lessons are received and assimilated.

If a team member does something wrong, but you never took the time to show them the right way, this problem is 100% your fault and not the employee's. You have to be willing to accept responsibility for your role. Once you have taught them or shown them how to do it, that's a different story. When an employee/co-worker lets you down, how you respond will determine the direction of your relationship with them and probably their future with your company.

Your choices are the same as with your kids:
- Yell at them, scold them and make them feel bad about themselves, hoping they won't do it again

or
- Use this as an opportunity to help grow yourself and them. Sit them down and have a conversation. Don't jump to conclusions or make assumptions. Listen to their side. Try to understand where they went wrong in their decision-making process.

Ask yourself:
- Did they have all the information they needed to make a better decision?
- Were they operating under the wrong assumptions?
- Is there something I haven't taught them yet that could have prevented this mistake?
- How can I, as the leader, put them on the correct path and ensure that they are clear about the proper expectations?
- Now that they have a clear understanding of what I expect, can I get a commitment from them to make the right decision next time?

- Are there any other systems or processes (SOPs) I can put in place, so this doesn't happen again?

> *"If you don't tell them what you want, you will not get the results you expect. It's your fault until they have been properly told and explained expectations."*
> ~ Matt Smith

Keep in mind that if you are new to this or learning a new way to handle positivity and discipline, it's like anything else. It takes repetition to create growth, so be consistent.

When you hear "No" to something that you want, your positivity is tested. People will focus on the "no" and get depressed, angry, or worse, give up. Don't Give UP! Instead…

Get past the NO's and find the YES! Remember: 'Yes' is a positive mindset.

"THE ANSWER IS YES. THE QUESTION IS HOW!"
~ Coach Dave Garcia

Be confident in your passion and stay focused. Not everyone will agree with your concepts or ideas, sometimes even your own family will doubt you, but if you feel in your heart that this decision is right, it probably is. Trust your gut and back it up with data, facts, and figures.

Do not get distracted by other people's thoughts or lack of belief in you. Believe in yourself to the finish line. Anyone successful has heard "NO," hundreds of times if not thousands, had sleepless nights and questioned their own decisions. That's all a part of the journey. Don't forget the old quote, "if it were easy, everyone would do it!"

> *"I've missed more than 9,000 shots in my career. I've lost almost 300 games. Twenty-six times I've been trusted to take the game-winning shot and missed. I've failed over and over and over again in my life. And that is why I succeed."*
>
> ~ Michael Jordan

When they tell you NO… and inevitably someone will WORK HARDER for the Yes! Do you know how many No's I heard when I decided to expand my Snap Fitness building? I listened to no from the bank, at least 50 times, and each time I knew that there had to be a way to find a yes. The project was a million dollars over budget. The banker suggested that I just buy the land around the project and wait until a better time to move forward. The banks didn't get it, so I had to keep convincing them that I knew what I was doing by taking this risk. My incredibly supportive wife saw the toll that this project was taking on me and like any caring partner had to ask, " Are you sure you want to keep going with this? Even with the cost overruns and the bankers trying to talk you out of it?" I wasn't turning back. I just kept pushing and convinced the bank to go through with it. I found a way to get the bank to say, "YES!" On May 1st, 2019, my Mom's birthday, we had our ribbon-cutting ceremony. The best decision of my life! The completed development project is a 4 million dollar building, the biggest Snap Fitness in the world, and a huge success.

Once the project completed, the banker shared that his stress level was off the charts for the entire duration. Seeing it all come to fruition, he and the rest of the bank now trust my judgment, vision, and decision-making ability. Don't be fooled into thinking that there is an end to the "No's." Even though the bank believes in me and my track record, other factors influence their lending decisions. This week, the bank told me to slow down and wait for the economy to level off before opening another Snooze Mattress location. This was their nice way of saying NO. My positivity keeps me believing that I'll always reach my goals, and this scenario is no different. So I met with another bank. I won't stop until I find a way to push forward with my vision because I know many more Snooze Mattress stores are coming!

I will never quit on me, and you should never quit on you!

"Numerous studies show that happy individuals are successful across multiple life domains, including marriage, friendship, income, work performance, and health."

Positivity leads to happiness. I notice that positive, happy people look for the good in everything and everyone around them. When a challenge or obstacle surfaces instead of being dragged down by it, positive people look for the silver lining in the lesson, and they keep going, finding a way over, around or through the obstacle. Choose positivity and use it as another technique in your life toolbox.

Negativity will knock the wind out of your sails; it will undermine you, and keep you from your goals and dreams. Negativity is stealthy. It creeps up on you, and you won't even realize that your default thoughts, feelings, and actions are rooted in negativity, but guess what, everyone else will notice it.

Don't wait another minute, do a self positivity check and work through the attack maneuvers below. GO GET YOUR POSITIVITY ON!

Positivity is a Muscle

Key Lesson Takeaways

- ✓ Self Positivity Check - pay attention to your words, thoughts, feelings, and actions
- ✓ Create a morning positivity workout routine
- ✓ Feed your positivity first (read, meditate, run, yoga, listen to podcasts or music)
- ✓ Read books to your children with positive messages
- ✓ Surround yourself with positive people
- ✓ Implement a News Fast to limit exposure to negativity

Jenny's Advice

Matt and I are two peas in a pod when it comes to positivity. Things won't always go your way. It's how you react to situations that make all the difference. Surround yourself with a tribe that is positive and inspires you to be the best version of yourself.

LESSON 3
*BEND*ing Time

Everyone has the same 24-hours a day. So how can you do more and get more out of the same amount of time? **You BEND it!**

Below are the components of the strategy I utilize to maximize my effectiveness every day. I organize my approach into four categories that give me a structure by which I can accomplish an incredible amount of tasks each day. While time is a constant when you employ my strategies, you might just feel like you're bending time.

Are you one of the 50% to 60% of dads who wish they could spend more time with their kids? If so, you'll find that using my system "Bend" will help you find ways to create the time you are craving.

Blueprint
Early
Nothing Wasted
Determination & Downtime

BEND - Blueprint

To control and manage time, you must build a blueprint for your day, week, and month. There are a variety of tools available out there that can help you organize your time. Some people like to see everything written out on a whiteboard or a paper calendar. Others use apps like Trello, Monday, To-Do Lists, or Task Manager. I use Google Calendar and Google Tasks on my phone, it's simple and always with me.

"Failing to plan is planning to fail"

~ Benjamin Franklin

An informative place to start is to take a snapshot of where and how you spend your time now. Be brutally honest with yourself on this because it won't help to "fudge" the figures. For instance, don't say that you spend x amount of time playing with the kids when, in reality, you spend that time surfing social media while your kids are watching cartoons or playing video games. On the work front, don't take credit for working extra hours if you spend a lot of those hours on personal calls or procrastination. Get real and see where your time is going.

If you don't know, then track it for a week. Most smartphones have the functionality to detail your usage by category. Using some of the tools in this book, your powers of observation, and technology (Toggle, RescueTime), you can quickly become aware of what you're doing now and shine a light on your areas of opportunity. This analysis can reveal how much time you spent on Productivity, Social Networking, Games, and specific apps. That will help you account for a large portion of your time. Zero in on your current habits, routines, attitudes, and approaches that may be contributing to your lack of success or balance in those areas you identified as opportunities.

Ask yourself, could my time be better allocated on more constructive endeavors? The point of this exercise is to understand how you are spending your time. Once you have a clear picture of where you are giving up precious time, you can become proactive and make adjustments geared toward helping you achieve your goals.

For example, if you are listening to music, playing video games, or watching TV for several hours a day, try cutting them in half. Start by reducing the time you occupy with these less productive pastimes and redirect some of it toward family, exercise, or productivity. I understand the need to have some chill time, me time, or do nothing time. I support the benefits of downtime because we all need to be re-energized; however, it's about balance. Make sure that you prioritize your goals and take responsibility for your results. Implementing this new program, you may find that you have replaced old behaviors with more beneficial activities that feed your growth instead of just filling your time. A marginal adjustment to your daily routine will make a dramatic change in your life.

Compare your results from the Defining and Aligning your Goals exercise in Chapter 1 The Power of Why, to the analysis you just completed on how you spend your time. You should now be able to identify how you are currently focusing your time and energy. This comparison is one more way to see with clarity where you excel and where you need to make some changes. This baseline will be beneficial as you start to set your action plan and schedule.

When setting your action plan, be sure to include goals and action steps that are specific, measurable, attainable, time-bound, and relevant. You want to be able to distinctly see how you are doing and when you are making progress. Prioritize your tasks and do the most important or difficult ones early in the day. Set time limits for specific activities so they won't chew up larger chunks and throw off your whole plan. Build buffers in your schedule in case the assignment takes longer than you think it will. Remember, Parkinson's Law tells us that work expands to fit the time allotted.

Another helpful tip is to color-code different types of activities or time blocks. Choose one color for business, one for family time, another for volunteer commitments, a different one for personal development, and so on. With color-coding, it's easier to see the portion of your schedule assigned to each category and make necessary adjustments for balance and priorities. One of the other benefits of color coding for me is the motivation factor. I use red for all of my current to-do items each day, especially my Top 3. As I complete it, I switch it to green, so I can see how much I have done and what's left to do. The goal is to get rid of the red every day.

In addition to getting yourself organized and scheduled on your calendar, it's essential also to add your kids' events to the schedule. Spend time regularly talking with your wife/partner and kids about what's on their calendars. I am very fortunate Jenny has always been a schedule-person, so I rely on her strength in this area. We discuss all the upcoming events (ie, school, sports, dance lessons, dentist appointments, clubs, committees, church group events). Consider your goals and priorities. Get it all mapped out, and be sure to plan for fun and family time. Try to think of everything. You can always adjust as you go along, but seeing the big picture when you're getting started is helpful. Don't forget to allocate time for planning.

Consistent routines can help save time and streamline the scheduling process. The blueprint phase is excellent to help you see, at a glance, everything that you need, and want to get done. Here is where you can assign priorities and find that balance between business and home. Not until you prioritize something as essential will you commit the time and follow through on it.

For example, Jenny and I feel it is super important for kids to have a routine around bedtime. We created this shared habit with our kids at a very early age. We put them to bed at 7:00 pm during the week and 7:30 pm on the weekend. Of course, you would adjust bedtime based on the age of your children. Consistency is the key to creating winning routines and habits. Since my kids know what to expect, they find a deep sense of comfort in this nightly routine. To help keep me on track, I regularly set the alarm on my phone to start the wind-down process. It works great!

When my alarm goes off, everyone knows they get a snack and one last show. Then it's the kids' bedtime when we read some books, pray and rub their backs and settle them into bed. The last part of putting the kids to bed is a review of each of their days. It helps all of us stay connected and in a place of gratitude. It's that exact sequence every single night; it does not waiver. If one of those pieces is missing, they'll tell me about it. One of the kids will say, "Dad, you didn't rub my back yet, or please don't forget to read the book." So they just know the routine, and it's a huge blessing because then we know they're in bed by 7:00 or 7:30 every night. Bedtime is something that our kids have fun with and enjoy. There's no drama or pleading to delay bedtime. My wife and I then have an hour together to hang out and talk about our days. We also recap our days by engaging in the 3-2-1-communication activity. We share three of the best things that happened today, the two worst and the one thing we are looking forward to for tomorrow. My family loves participating in the 3-2-1 conversation technique. I cover it in more detail in the chapter titled: Art Of Better Communication with this 321 Technique.

It seems simple, but I see many parents who don't have a bedtime schedule for their kids. I couldn't even imagine that, because I think it's something you want to instill as early as possible. I know kids who are the same age as my kids who stay up until midnight or later. Those parents say they can't get them to bed. That creates stress for both the children and the parents. I also know couples who don't carve out any couple time at the end of the day. Couple time is vital for healthy relationships and families.

If you have begun to blueprint your time, you might be amazed by how much you are already doing and how the tools I'm sharing with you will help you achieve even more throughout your days. You might be surprised to find out just what it took for me to become successful.

In the transition time, where you may be now when I shifted my focus from being a diligent hard worker for someone else's company and growing my enterprise on the side to now setting my schedule and running several successful businesses, my days looked very different.

Before I technically retired, my typical day was a sprint to the finish line day in and day out. I worked for someone else in retail sales as a commission employee. To be as successful in retail sales as I was, I worked every chance I could from open to close. As a young single man, I was a night owl, didn't pay much attention to my diet, or think much about my overall health. I would get up around 7 am and get to work by 9 am. I spent my time as follows:

- Worked seven days a week
- 12 hours for five days a week - working retail for someone else
- 4 hours working those same five days, growing my businesses

My two days off were spent at Snap Fitness, working my business. Somehow I spent time with friends and traveling.

Like you, I was juggling many things all at once. I was driven and focused and working non-stop. How did I manage this crazy pace? Life is a balancing act, and I hope to offer you my tips on finding your balance.

The long hours of those early days taught me how to squeeze every ounce out of my days. You cannot create more time, but you can bend it. I learned to leverage every second of the day and to waste nothing.

I found ways to multitask that didn't detract from any of my responsibilities; I call it "Smart-Tasking." During my lunch breaks, I would go on an estimate for my carpet cleaning business, schedule volunteer, community, and other business meetings outside of my retail job. In retail, there are often long gaps between customers. Unlike many of my colleagues who played games or relaxed, I was returning voicemails, setting up appointments, brainstorming, and researching ways to grow my businesses. I gave 100% every day for each job.

To my surprise, once I married and had my children, my priorities shifted. I realized that I need to be healthy so I can live a long life to be part of my children's lives as they grow up, be there for every moment, creating great memories. I want to meet my grandchildren and great-grandchildren. To do this, I had to find a different balance to my days, so I overhauled my schedule. I am no longer a night owl. I now get up at 4:30 am; I exercise and am more conscious of what I eat. I have a new sense of determination as I now focus my energy on longevity.

Are you in this same place in life? Do you also need to shift your schedule? Perhaps you've realized that you want to have more time with your family. Let's look at my current calendar to see how my priorities have changed and how I make time for family and business.

As you know, I retired in my 30's. No, I don't live on the beach or lay around in a hammock all day. My definition of retirement is that I no longer work for someone else. This shift means I now choose how my day is structured, what businesses I build, what dreams I pursue, and how I spend time with my family. I own my time. Having control over my time was the main reason that this was such a significant goal for me. I know what it meant to me as a kid to not have a dad around for any of my ball games or choir practices. I vowed that I would be there for all of my kids' activities. My retirement means that I don't have to miss any baseball or football games, dance recitals, or spontaneous trips with my family. I even have enough time now that I am coaching them in sports. Can you imagine owning your time? It's a game-changer!

Everything I do is for my family. If you remember one thing about this book or me, I value and put Family First.

I still put in long days. There are three main differences. First, I get up super early, so my day starts long before my family is even awake. Second, using the strategies in this book, I maximize every second of every day. Third, I am living my dream life because this approach allows me the total freedom to create my schedule so that I never miss any family time.

Now

On a typical weekday, I go to bed around 8:30 or 9 pm to wake up somewhere around 4:30 every morning. Getting eight hours of quality sleep is essential to me; after all, I'm a mattress guy. Once I wake up, I have my pre-workout supplement to get myself moving. Depending on the season, I either run outside, weight train, or use cardio equipment and put on an audiobook and go for an hour.

Until last year, I hated running. Completing a marathon was on my bucket list for 2019, so I made it a personal challenge. When I first began training, I had to make myself start running, but now I love to put on my shoes and go. I put on some music, a book, or a podcast. I get my mind and body fired up and pumping. It gets my mental state where I need it to be.

Right now, I'm reading two different books on Audible. In addition to the workout time, I will read or listen to books throughout the morning, and listen to podcasts. I enjoy podcasts and motivational videos. They might relate to what's going on in my life or what I may be researching. No matter what it is, as long as you're feeding positivity into your brain as early as possible, you are starting your day off right. When you stimulate your mind in this way, two things happen; first, you have told your brain to focus on being positive for the day, and secondly, your brain releases hormones that allow you to be more productive and happier throughout the day. Giving yourself this kind of time every day will enable you to grow exponentially. That's how I spend the first 60-90 minutes of every day. Try this for yourself, and you, too, will quickly see significant shifts mentally and physically. Learning and fitness are critical to personal and professional growth.

After my workout, I grab my laptop, see what's going on, and immediately tackle whatever is critical. I might send a reminder email to the team about things we need to do that day or something I thought about the night before. I am a big believer in showing appreciation, so I make time to send out recognition and gratitude emails from the previous day's successes. I spend time each week connecting with people in my life. I think it's valuable to get a pulse check, see how everybody is doing, and find out if there is something I can do for them. I review my plan for the day and make any needed adjustments. I prepare myself for the day by asking, "What's on my schedule today? When are my meetings? What are the goals for the day and week? Are we on track? What do my kids need? What does my wife need?" I also review any additional reminders I may have jotted down the night before.

Along the way, I will quickly check the news and social media to see what's going on in the world. Remember, you're following a schedule that you've created, so be true to yourself in terms of how much time you spend on social media. It's too easy to get drawn into the social media trap and lose track of time. With my ADD, I can get sucked in pretty quick, and the next thing I'm asking myself, "why am I watching a ninja dog video?" There are apps for your phone that will limit the amount of time you spend on social media. You can set the parameters, and it will shut you down after that amount of time. It can save you from losing large chunks of valuable time.

Everybody else in my house starts moving around seven(ish). I have breakfast with the kids and spend a little bit of time with them, getting them dressed and ready for the day. Some mornings we watch a few minutes of cartoons or play games. Lately, we've been playing a lot of board games, and we've been doing these cool Lego projects. We finished a project the other day that had about 900 or 1,000 pieces. We also have some wood building projects. We stimulate and challenge our kids as much as possible through different types of building projects, board games, and sports.

During the school year, I typically drop the kids off around 8:00 am. When they're on summer break, I take them to the YMCA day camp each morning.

I'm an avid believer in the benefits of coaches and mentors. I incorporate and use the expertise of others as part of my weekly schedule. I have several coaches in my life, including a coach for business, fitness, social media, marriage, and life. I even have two coaches specifically for this book. If it's a Monday, I have coaching calls from 8:00 to 9:00 am and 1:00 to 2:00 pm where my experts are helping me raise my game to the next level. During these sessions, we discuss what's going on in each business, focus on three major priorities, brainstorm a game plan, and commit to getting them done. I highly recommend that you consider a coach or mentor; you'll quickly view them as an integral part of your success.

After the call, I head over to the brick and mortar store and start the next phase of my day. I am disciplined enough that I follow the schedule that I've created. Of course, you must be flexible to adapt to surprises and last-minute changes. I make sure that I prepare for meetings and other previously scheduled activities. For each of my different businesses, I conduct a daily management meeting, check the financials, and run a weekly staff meeting. Some days I am putting out fires, but most of the time, because I have built the right team and implemented effective systems, I can focus on what's next in the big picture or long-range plan and on team development.

On a recent day, this 9-5 "work time block" included:

- Looking at real estate for an expansion project
- Reviewing daily sales results and creating role-play based on missed opportunities
- Quick check-in call with my wife
- Equip, Excite, and Energize working lunch with the team
- Metro Board Meeting
- Emails to experts and research on optimal size and layout for building
- Coaching call
- Plan calendar and to-do's for next day
- Walkthrough and last checks on businesses
- Wrap up the workday

Spending time with my children is a priority; therefore, it is essential to plan my day to capitalize on every moment and opportunity. To be fully present with my children, at 5 pm I have to switch gears. I take off my work hat and put on my dad hat. I am in dad mode for the remainder of the night. This routine is my way of achieving a balance between work and home. I also dedicate my weekends to my family. There are times when I have a Pueblo West Metropolitan Board Meeting (like City Council but we are not quite a city yet) or volunteer commitment, but I try to minimize their impact on our family time. Be diligent about sticking to your schedule and not allowing work to invade your family time. It's a slippery slope. If you have to make an exception, adjust other parts of your schedule to rebalance the time distribution. After returning from a work trip, I take time off to catch-up with my family.

Once the kids are in bed and after my wife and I catch up, I take a minute to jot down a few things that I want to tackle the next morning.

Take the time to blueprint your life onto your calendar and prioritize what is most important. This groundwork will set you up for success with both work and family, and whatever time it takes will be well worth the balance and productivity that you gain in your life. You'll find your stress levels decreasing because you have a plan that you can follow, things will stop falling through the cracks.

Monday - Friday At a Glance:

BENDing Time - Daily Routine
Monday - Friday at a glance

Time	Task
8:30 PM	(The night before) - go to bed
4:30 AM	Get up
4:30 AM - 6:00 AM	Pre-workout supplement, cardio while listening to an audiobook or podcast
6:00 AM - 7:00 AM	Grab my laptop - email and research
7:00 AM - 8:00 AM	Spend time with kids - breakfast, get them ready for the day
8:00 AM	Drop kids off at school
8:00 AM - 9:00 AM	Coaching calls (business coach, life coach, fitness trainer)
9:00 AM	Head to the office
9:00 AM - 5:00 PM	Staff and manager meetings, daily operations, business development, big picture and brainstorming
5:00 PM	Switch hats - end business day / resume Dad mode - pick up kids
5:00 PM - 7:30 PM	Quality time with family
7:30 PM - 8:30 PM	Quality time with wife
8:30 PM	Take Melatonin and go to bed with meditation music

Weekends - Family Adventure Time

Weekends - Family Adventure Time

My schedule might not be what yours will look like, so below, I am providing a high-level outline that you can use for arranging your week. Organizing your days and weeks will become second nature once you are consistent with your planning. Modify your calendar so that it fits your family and work needs, and be sure to leave time for last-minute challenges or adventures!

Monday	Meet with Coaches and Advisors
Tuesday	Meet with the leadership of your organizations
Wednesday	Dedicate 1-on-1 time with staff and family – Focus this time to build these relationships
Thursday	Big Picture Planning in the morning
Friday	All hands-on-deck-meeting. The team brings ideas, and we discuss the "good's, bad's, and ugly's." Pinpoint where you are so you know where you are going. Create clarity of vision for the team and your family. Plan the week and Enter items into your calendar system.
Saturday	Family Time
Sunday	Family Time

My current schedule is a gift. Create a strategy that allows you to focus on family and business and makes you feel good about you.

To recap, you have to plan everything from when you wake up to when you go to bed and everything in between. Why? If you don't, things will get missed, and you already know how that feels. I want you to be successful, wildly successful, in your businesses, and with your family. You can't have excuses. You must have a plan, and you must follow that plan.

BEND – Early

"Take on the day, or the day will take you on."

~ Matt Smith

Studies have shown that more than half of self-made millionaires wake up three hours before their workday begins. Richard Branson, Gary Vaynerchuk, Warren Buffett, Elon Musk, Jeff Bezos, and Mark Zuckerberg all get up early to get a head start. How could their early morning rituals help you to be happy, healthy, and hugely successful?

Here's what they do in the morning.

Exercise - increases energy level, sparks a positive attitude

Meditation - reduces stress, enhances creativity, sharpens focus

Plan - clarifies goals, prioritizes tasks

Read - broadens knowledge base, provides differing perspectives

Tackle Most Important or Most Difficult Task - creates a sense of accomplishment and relief

Quality Time with Family / Friends - improves relationships, provides health benefits

**(from The Start Up, Medium's Largest Entrepreneurship Publication, written by Steve Spring, August 12, 2019, "Inspiring Morning Routines of Highly Successful People").

This concept was one of my most crucial mindset shifts, and one of the biggest keys to my success. I made this change in the last few years because it struck me as fundamental if I wanted to achieve my vision for my life. I admire this trait in the entrepreneurs listed above. I decided that if they do it, so will I, and when I make a decision, I dive in and do it.

I am still amazed at how much more productive I have been from these bonus hours. At this hour, there are very few distractions while my family is still asleep and my phone never rings. It is mind-blowing how much I can conquer early in the morning. Talk about bending time. It sets up your whole day for success because you are supercharged by getting a jumpstart each morning.

> Okay, so now you are thinking, "Man, how do I get up two or three hours earlier? I'm already putting in a long day."

Here are two options to help you achieve this. One

way is to take the plunge. You just set the alarm two or three hours earlier on day one, knowing you might be tired later in the day, but you are so committed to your goal that you will power through it. The other way is to gradually shift your wake-up time by 30 minutes at a time, giving yourself a few days to adjust to this new daily routine before the next shift. Doing it the second way, you will gain the two or three hours in a couple of weeks. It's no surprise that I am a fan of extremes, so I went all-in on day one. Either way, you do it, you will be glad you did when you see how productive you can be with this time. It can take some time to turn a new behavior into a habit, and the process isn't an all or nothing. So if you miss one day, you don't have to lose all your momentum. Just get up early the next day. Stick with the early wake-up times until it becomes something you look forward to because the benefits are so rewarding. For a little extra help getting up, check out the 5 second rule for getting out of bed by Mel Robbins. It's simple - don't hit the snooze button! I found it very useful.

Just getting up early isn't enough. If you just wake up early, you might be tired and tempted to go back to bed. You have to have a plan of action to set yourself up for success. Have a purpose and a goal each morning. I use this time to get some form of fitness, feed my brain, and work for a few hours. You could work out, read or listen to a book, meditate, write love letters, listen to podcasts, or brainstorm an invention. If you plan to read or listen to a book or podcast, be efficient, and have it already downloaded onto your phone, tablet, or laptop. Nourish your brain with valuable and pertinent information, and you will expand your mind. What you put into your consciousness is what you get out. As you improve the quality of the information you're consuming today, it will lead to tomorrow's path of success. You will feel like your brain is an idea machine; you might even notice that your visions are reaching beyond what you ever have thought possible.

Another way to maximize this early morning time while the rest of the house is quiet is to spend a few minutes the day before to plan out a Top 3 List. This list focuses on those things that you need to accomplish to move you towards your business goals, relationships, family, finances, body, and mind. Ask yourself, what is the next step you need to take in each area? Update your calendar to include your daily Top 3. Completing these tasks gives you the wins you need that day to be a success. Base your daily priorities on your primary objectives. If you can just commit to 3 significant accomplishments per day, that's 90 major wins a month, and more than 1,000 wins a year! **It only takes three per day**!

Another thing that I have recently learned that helps me make the most of my bonus hours is to leave my phone on airplane or Do Not Disturb mode during this time.

Try this simple tip to stay focused so that you won't get distracted by phone calls, social media, or emails, etc.

You don't want to start replying to emails at 4:30 am because that's not why you're waking up this early. That completely defeats the purpose. Stay focused on using this time for developing you. Take at least the first hour or two to better you today and in the future

However you choose to use this time, you need to plan and execute it every day. You have just given yourself almost 100 hours of uninterrupted bonus time every month, an additional 2.5 weeks, which is incredibly powerful! Do something amazing with this gift!

Imagine what you can accomplish with an additional 5-6 months every year!!

"Today is going to be a good day because you are going to make it a good day!"

~ Matt Smith

Even though I have prepared the whole day and logged it in the calendar, so I have a plan for the next day, as I close my eyes to sleep, something will pop into my brain. I will quickly grab my phone and type in a reminder. It could be a short message like "send an appreciation email for what somebody did today," or it could be, "fill out this application" because I forgot and then let it slip from my mind. Jotting these quick reminders allows me to let go of nagging thoughts so I can sleep more deeply.

Although our bodies produce it naturally, I take melatonin every night to help shut my brain off. Check with your physician before you try any supplements. I've also been working on an invention that will incorporate the ocean's calming sounds to improve dreaming habits. Stay tuned for this invention. It's going to change the sleeping game! When you dream, your brain is integrating, processing, and harnessing your subconscious mind to work on solutions to the problems you focused on during the day.

Mark Twain once said, "If it's your job to eat a frog, it's best to do it first thing in the morning. And if it's your job to eat two frogs, it's best to eat the biggest one first." Not a pretty sight, but you get the point. You have more energy and focus in the morning, so it's the best time to tackle your most difficult or demanding tasks. Checking that item off your to-do list will give you a massive sense of accomplishment that will fuel your momentum for the rest of the day.

BEND - Nothing Wasted

There is a balancing act between double-dipping or "smart-tasking" and being 100% present in the moment you are with and what you are doing. I'm not advising that you multitask. Multitasking involves dividing your attention across two or more tasks. The University of Michigan found a 20% - 40% decrease in productivity when undertaking many things at one time. Instead, I use what I call Smart-Tasking, which is being creative in finding the time to get things done. I can guarantee my wife has no idea how much I work when she's not watching because that's my strategy. If it does not affect her or the family time, then I'm winning. Jenny enjoys many activities that are her own. One example, believe it or not, is she loves gardening. She says it's almost meditative, getting close to nature, and there's a real sense of accomplishment when she's done. It seems to bring her great joy. I try to take full advantage of this time to catch up with other items on my to-do list. Visits to the bathroom are a good time to respond quickly to a message or email.

My best secret for bending time is this: I look for little opportunities throughout the day to maximize my productivity. It's like finding loose change. It might not seem like much by itself, but a minute or two here and there used wisely can absolutely add up in terms of what you get done in a day, and it can save you a big chunk of time by the end of the week. Here are some Smart-Tasking ideas:

- Work out and listen to a book on self-development or business principles
- Respond to a quick work text while you are on hold
- Prepare for the next day when your kids are sleeping
- Check or respond to email while you wait for everyone to show up for a meeting
- Research your business competition when you are waiting for dinner to finish cooking
- Build your brand on Social Media while you wait at the doctor's office

- Use commute time for podcasts, audiobooks, phone calls for work or to connect with family and friends
- Send voice messages or dictate texts with apps like Voxer[1] or WhatsApp
- Use an App called Pocket to save Website or Blog articles, then read them in line at the grocery store ...
- Let's be honest; everyone spends time in the bathroom. Respond to a quick text message or email
- Instead of driving to work, walk, run or cycle and listen to a podcast - TRIPLE DIP

The possibilities are endless. Be creative DOUBLE DIP, but also remember to be 100% present. Look for little gaps of time then use this loose change to win big.

The human brain can only focus for about 90-minute at a time, so consider this when planning out your blocks of time for various activities.

Mix it up a little. After a meeting, go for a short walk or other activity before sitting down to jump into your next task. This variety will allow you a proper transition, to

---

[1] Side note about Voxer - for me, it has been a game-changer! It's a way of having a conversation with multiple people but at your convenience in terms of timing. I have at least 20 group chats going all the time (ie, Snooze, Carpet Cleaning, Snap, front desk, warehouse, sales, friends, family) When one person asks a question like, Hey, Matt, what are your thoughts on this customer situation? I can record a quick answer, and instantly the entire team has the information, and we are all on the same page. It saves me from having to answer the same question multiple times. It also sparks some great brainstorming and problem solving among the teams.

shift gears and clear your mind of one thing before you start in on the next. Taking a walk or doing some other form of movement will pump more oxygen to the brain, reinvigorating it and effectively stimulating overall blood flow that may have slowed during the previous stint of sitting.

Learn correct prioritization so you can focus most of your efforts on the duties that will yield the most and best results. There are many different approaches to sorting and prioritizing your daily assignments and a variety of Apps to manage the process. The crucial thing to realize is that not all tasks on your to-do list are equal. Some items on your list are an undeniable high priority and will yield significant results. These tend to be things like actual emergencies, deadline-driven activities, preparation and planning, relationship building, or pressing problems. Other items are neither very important nor urgent. They often include junk mail, mindless TV watching, or random social media scrolling. Your job is to identify and eliminate the time-wasters from your day and focus your best efforts on productive things that keep you moving forward in all areas of your life.

When planning out your daily schedule, group similar tasks together into a single time block to minimize the time it takes to switch gears. You will be far more efficient when you focus your mind on a particular set of 'like' activities. For instance, read and respond to emails only at specific times during the day rather than stopping what you are doing every time something comes into your inbox. Gallup and The Institute for Future both estimate that we are interrupted every ten minutes by communication technologies such as email and text. Once disrupted, it can take an average of 25 minutes from that distraction to get fully back on task, according to a study by Gloria Mark at the University of California, Irvine.

Stick to the calendar and watch out for time leakage, when tasks spill over into the next time slot. Adhering to your agenda is most important. I am as guilty as anybody that if I have a meeting planned for half an hour, I can go for two hours because I am a people person. I sincerely care and want to know about your life and your family. I had to train myself to stay on topic and block out time for those more in-depth conversations outside of the meeting.

Save time and money by getting and staying organized. The average person loses a ridiculous amount of time and money looking for items they have misplaced. Newsweek states this wasted time can be almost one full hour per day at home, and according to OrganizedWorld.com, an additional hour and a half per day at work. What could you do with an extra 2.5 hours per day? If you spend the time to arrange your workspace, office, home, and car once and completely, it is much easier to stay organized. When there is a designated place for each item to be, you know, at a glance, if your supply of frequently used items is getting low, and it's quicker at the end of your work sessions to clean up and put things away. Another area where you can spin your wheels is searching for documents you have created and can't remember where you filed them. To avoid this, develop and or follow a document management system on your computer and be consistent. Keep a quick reference guide for the path to the most frequently used documents or create a shortcut on your desktop.

Would it surprise you to learn that the average business leader spends approximately 21.8 hours per week on low-value activities? ** That's almost three full workdays every week! This lost time is a perfect reason to bend time through delegation. It can be hard to think about handing over specific tasks to anyone else, but many can generally be done by someone else in your organization or family. To our surprise, in many cases, they can do it better or faster than we can, especially if they have a natural talent or expertise in that skillset. The hack here is being able to identify strengths and opportunities for yourself and your team accurately. My best advice is to surround yourself with individuals who are smarter than you and more adept in the areas you are not. This approach makes the system work best. It's crucial to choose where you spend your time and trust your team with other responsibilities.

I know entrepreneurs who say they can't expand because they don't trust their employees to show up, be honest, and take care of their customers. If you are reluctant to trust your team and feel like you have to do it all yourself, then you need to:

- Look at who and how you hire and train - Trust your team
- Build systems to promote honesty, reliability and customers service
- When something goes wrong, learn from it, re-evaluate your hiring and systems, close the loophole, then MOVE ON

Anything you do more than once, record the process, and create a system for it.

Invest the effort to develop systems that teach one or more people to do a particular task or set of tasks. What you save in the long run will pay you dividends for years to come. This fact is particularly accurate of routine or repetitive jobs that do not require your specific attention. If you don't have the resources to train someone on your team to do the activities, maybe consider hiring an independent contractor or virtual assistant who can pick up specific assignments, as you need them done. This change will free you up to focus on the tasks that truly require your attention.

Telecommuting or working from home has many advantages. The key is motivation. COVID-19 has completely changed the way I view my day. I will never go back to spending 40 hours a week in the office. Over these past several weeks of the quarantine, I've learned that I can get more work done and do a better job balancing family and business, working from home at least part of the day. My day is more fluid, and I am closer to family activities. There's also less downtime as I transition from work to home. I am more present for my family, giving Jenny a break throughout the day by caring for our kids. Our family bonds are growing stronger each day.

My associates are working together remotely. Our interactions have become more creative and have allowed us to connect and grow as individuals and as a team. This forced shutdown has helped shift my focus from the small picture day-to-day running of the businesses to redefining my role in each company. When we reopen, I will delegate more responsibilities to my capable co-workers. They will appreciate the growth opportunities and recognition, and I will concentrate on creating a more expanded vision of my future.

Profit from the bending time concept of "nothing wasted" by capturing lost time and finding loose change to sneak in extra productivity without making your day any longer. When you employ this technique, your businesses and family will benefit, and you will experience a sense of relief and satisfaction, knowing that you squeeze every bit of goodness out of your day. There's nothing quite like laying your head on your pillow at the end of one of these days, knowing you mastered the day.

* (Inc., "New Study Shows You're Wasting 21.8 Hours a Week" by David Finkel)

BEND - Determination/Downtime

> "Last year, my husband decided to run a marathon and mind you he was not a runner and had never run over 2 miles in his life. He signed up for a half marathon. A few minutes into the race, he called me and asked if I would be okay to hang out a few more hours for him to finish the entire marathon, all 26.2 miles. Without any real training, he completed it!.
>
> He goes big and gives everything 100%! That is why I admire him"
>
> Jenny Smith

When the weekend rolls around, what choice do you make?

- Sleep in, watch Netflix, chill with some games, or
- Get up, Get moving and Charge forward to your goals

Let's face it; most of us will go along enduring the status quo even though we are not happy or fully satisfied until we reach the tipping point. The tipping point is where the pain and frustration of where you are, exceed the perceived pain and effort of doing something different. The bottom line here is you have to want to make a change then commit to doing the work to make the adjustments that will lead you to a more abundant and balanced life. Big goals start with small decisions. If getting started is the hardest part, then keeping it going is the next important step toward success.

You picked up this book to improve some aspect of your life. Now we need to talk about the underlying force that drives all of this – YOU! Here is where the test of your determination comes into play. I want you to WIN BIG! But you are the only one who can make winning your reality.

> **"Discipline is simply choosing between what you want now and what you want most."**
> ~ Dr Ann Vertel, Psychologist, Retired Navy Officer, Corporate Trainer

Much like any other modification in your daily routine, you have to get strict with yourself and embrace the new system. Accept NO excuses! I know a lot of people, especially here in Colorado, who will say, "Oh, it's snowing outside, so I'm not going running." They'll bag the entire workout just because they could not execute their plan exactly as they thought. Be creative and find the "yes" answer from yourself. If you can't run outside, go downstairs and do push-ups, sit-ups, curls, and whatever else you can think of to make up your workout. Don't make or accept the excuse. Follow through and stick to your plan. That's a big part of why fitness training for people is so helpful. A trainer is someone who holds you accountable and pushes you to expand your limits. Even though I have been in the fitness industry for more than 13 years, and I know what to do when I go to the gym,

I pay a trainer to push me and hold me accountable. For so many people, that is a missing element. Business coaches are instrumental to me for the same reason. They provide extra accountability that keeps me on track and focused on my plan to achieve my goals. I have several coaches, and my wife, to assist. Is there someone in your life that will help keep you honest? Someone you can regularly check in with quickly to act as your accountability partner?

Determination is the discipline that will propel you from where you are now towards your best life. According to the dictionary, determination is "firmness of purpose." Meaning that nothing will cause you to waiver from taking the necessary steps to achieve your vision. If you remember, we started by initially discussing The Power Of Why. Here is where you'll discover if your why is strong enough to keep you moving toward your goals. A powerful why is the motivating force that allows you to persevere, day in and day out, overcoming obstacles and staying the course.

Since the time of Aristotle, grit has been recognized and revered. According to Psychologist Angela Lee Duckworth, in a recent TED talk called "The Strongest Predictor of Success", "the most significant predictor of success is not social intelligence, good looks, physical health, or IQ. It is grit! Grit is passion and perseverance for very long-term goals, … having stamina, … sticking with your future, … day in day out for years, … and working really hard to make that future a reality."

I'm not asking you to do anything that I haven't done. Right here, right now, I am asking that you dig deep and find your grit!

In March 2018, I made one of the gutsiest moves I have ever made in business and life. I quit my job! That may not sound like a bold move until you hear the rest of the story. I gambled everything on my grit. I loved my job, loved going to work every day, and brought home a solid six-figure income. I had a growing family to support, multiple mortgages, and was in the middle of creating the largest Spa in southern Colorado. Simultaneously, I was constructing the largest Snap Fitness facility in the world. The Snap construction project was a personal dream; I fought very hard and pushed daily to see it come to life.

The bank rejected my building loan application several times before I finally squeaked through the approval process. My stable income and a detailed strict budget were the deciding factors. Things will often go wrong on a project of this magnitude, and my four million dollar project was one million dollars over budget. Securing tenants for the commercial space became even more critical. Halfway through the project, I decided I had to leave my job of 18 years. I wanted to focus on working for me and structuring my time so that I could put my family first. I knew I needed to take this leap of faith and never look back. Of course, I never told the bank of my plans to leave behind my significant salary, which I used to secure the loan approval. You probably think I was crazy, but that's how leaps of faith work. For me, family first means that I'm willing to risk everything to give my family the life they deserve. I believed in my grit, gut, and determination and knew that I would find a way to make it work. It was now or never and never wasn't an option! At that moment, I became a Dad-prenuer.

Do you have grit? Are you determined? How have you persevered? When asked these questions, most people will conjure up memories of some painful or tragic event to show that they have survived and come through the other side victorious. Grit isn't only for negative or traumatic versions of life. Let's flip the narrative. You have a vision and goals; how you get there is up to you. You can be positive or negative about your journey. You can see your path full of obstacles, or you can envision helpers along the way.

> "Whether you think you can, or you think you can't – you're right."

This famous quote by Henry Ford highlights that determination and grit are about mental fortitude. I believe so strongly in the power of positivity, I have dedicated an entire chapter to it.

If you don't think grit comes naturally to you, don't worry. You can build it through the repetition of small victories and by creating the habits that support dedication. Determination starts with knowing your Why. That constant is your underlying motivation. On top of that, you layer your unwavering belief in your ability to achieve your goals, based on all the little wins in your life. It doesn't hurt to sprinkle in a dose of inspiration or courage then wrap it up in positivity. Now, you have a recipe for grit!

As with everything in life, there is a balance that we strive to achieve. Balance is not static; it's not something achieved and completed. It is a dynamic state of being. We always weigh our priorities and goals and make adjustments to create the life we desire and deserve.

Are you familiar with Newton's Third Law? It states, "For every action, there is an equal and opposite reaction." Said another way, "Work hard, play harder!" You can't work full-tilt every day indefinitely. The human body cannot sustain such a demanding pace while maintaining optimal health. Similarly, both the human spirit and mind also need recharging. Allocating time for recreation rest and recuperation are essential to achieving those long stretches of high performance.

Even in my early days, when I was running full out all the time, juggling so many hats and working what felt like 24/7, I was also rewarding myself and keeping my sanity by making time to travel and stay connected with my friends, and having a social life. Now, with my significantly modified schedule, my days stacked and productive, I sustain that pace for concentrated periods. Then my family and I take some much-deserved downtime. We make frequent short trips to our mountain home and more extended vacations to explore the world.

When I was 17 years old, my dad took me on a cruise; it was also the first time I owned a suit. That holiday sparked my passion for travel. Whenever I have time, I explore the world. I am fortunate enough to afford family vacations, getaways with just my wife, special one-on-one times with my kids, and even guys trips. We also visit our cabin in the mountains twice a month. I have realized that the cabin we love is reminiscent of when my mom would take my brother and me to these mountains. Those outings with her were such formative parts of my life. I am grateful for the beautiful lessons I learned from my mother and still hold in my heart.

These downtimes allow my brain and body to reset. They are how I balance my intense schedule. The greatest gifts are the memories that I make with my family and friends. I hope that you, too, can make lasting memories like the ones I have created. While traveling is one of my favorites, you should find ways to reward yourself, your friends, and your family with whatever interests you.

You now understand the importance of crafting a Blueprint for success by planning out your day, week, and month. You have learned that getting up earlier gives you an advantage that accelerates your growth. You have several examples of how you can squeeze even more productivity into your day, so you don't waste any time. Finally, remember that YOU are the most significant factor in your own success story. Keep your Why in the front of your mind, and access your determination to form new habits, fuel your growth and success. Great job for embracing all of these lessons!!

Strive for excellence, not perfection.

"Excellence is achievable; perfection is a matter of opinion."

~ Judy Halish

*BEND*ing Time

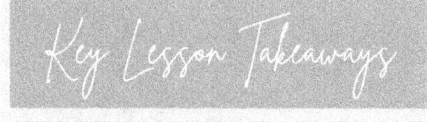

- ✓ *Blueprint* - Complete the worksheets to develop your calendar/plan for the week (click below for template)
- ✓ *Early* - Get up two to three hours earlier each day and plan out what you will do with this bonus time, Don't hit Snooze! (attached checklist will give you some great ideas to get started)
- ✓ *Nothing Wasted* - Look for the "loose change," small pockets of time for short tasks to increase efficiency, and use "Smart Tasking" to maximize your time. Download and start using Voxer to communicate with work-groups and family.
- ✓ *Determination/Downtime* - Get clear on your WHY, Find your Grit, Commit, Reward, and Recharge yourself with rest, relaxation, and fun. (Use the attached worksheet to complete the Defining and Aligning your Goals Exercise from chapter 1)

Download your workbook here: cerealdadpreneur.com/bookbonuses

Jenny's Advice

Holy cow, Batman, our lives are busy! Matt gets up early every morning, hours before all of us, to start *Bend*ing time. I believe this is why he is so successful at everything he does. Find a scheduling system you can share. Communicate all updates and changes with each other. You both have to be on the same page.

LESSON 4

Two Ears, One Mouth - Art Of Better Communication

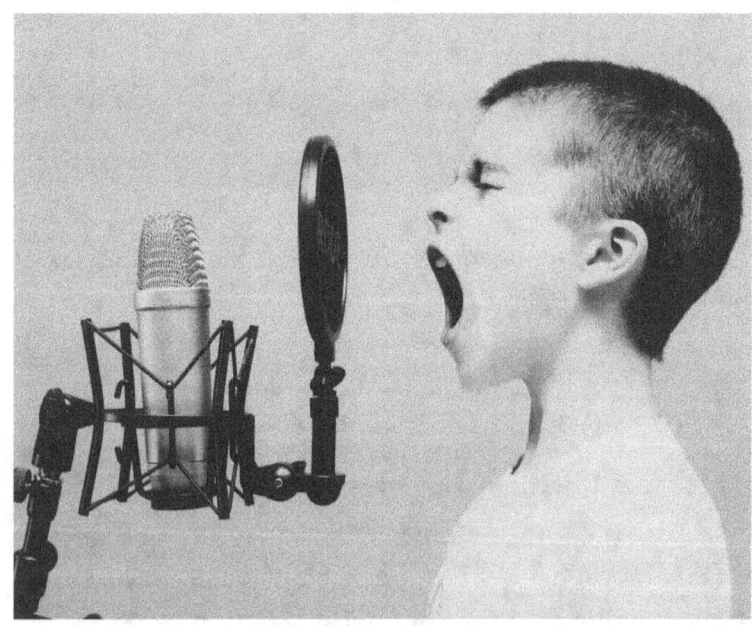

Photo by Jason Rosewell on Unsplash

> "Communication is the key for success in all relationships, businesses, and parenting. Always sharpen this skill"
>
> ~ Matt Smith

Communication is the information highway that connects people and forms the foundation for any lasting, healthy relationship. Both at home and at work, I have created a culture where communication is open, honest, and from the heart. Support for this culture is evident at all levels of my organizations and through every member of my family. Everyone participates, and we hear each voice. Your family and your employees need to know that you view them as valuable. Whether you are at work or home, give your full attention to whomever you're engaging with, so they can feel how much you genuinely care.

Good listening is essential for effective communication and can build rapport and trust in a relationship or in groups. We have all heard the familiar expression, "You have two ears and only one mouth," but have you ever stopped to think about how that applies to excellent communication? Of course, the meaning of this message is that we can often contribute more to a conversation, and learn more about a person or situation when we listen and allow others to speak, more than when we dominate the conversation. As leaders in a business organization, family unit, or community group, listening is a fundamental skill for success. Good listening is more than just hearing the words that are said, and it is more than waiting for your turn to talk.

Active listening requires that you genuinely listen with caring intent to witness and more fully understand the person who is speaking. If it doesn't come naturally, active listening is a skill that you can develop. It also involves using your other senses and comes from a non-judgmental, honestly empathetic state of being. The listener observes the non-verbal cues such as body language and eye contact and pays particular attention to the word choice. For example, is the speaker using words like "I feel …" or "I think …?" In an active listening exchange, the listener will often paraphrase to summarize what they have heard to demonstrate or confirm that they have a clear understanding of what the speaker is sharing. The listener can also show their attention through their body language, leaning forward, nodding, and facial expressions that convey concern or interest, reserving any judgment of what is being said.

In my family, we always make sure we take the time to talk. We plan out our weeks, share our hopes and dreams, discuss what bothers each of us, and my wife, Jenny, and

I figure out how we can help our children with whatever challenge they are facing.

One of the ways that we foster meaningful conversations is with an engaging exercise taught to me by one of my coaches. It is something he calls 3-2-1, and it only takes a few minutes. I've heard that other successful families use a similar activity called the Rose, Thorn, and Buds format. It is so effective that my wife and I have incorporated it into our daily rituals. This family activity works wonderfully around the dinner table or as part of your bedtime routine. Each member of the family takes turns describing their Roses, Thorns, and Buds. Roses are the best part of your day. Thorns are the worst part of your day, and Buds are what you are looking forward to tomorrow. In the case of the 3-2-1 Exercise, we share three achievements or successes of the day, two challenges of the day, and one thing you look forward to tomorrow or later in the week. Because of the age of my kids, I pose the questions as:

- "What did you like best about today?"
- "What did you not like about today?"
- "What are you looking forward to for tomorrow?"

We originally began using this exercise during dinner with our kids and recently switched to doing it with them just before bed. Incorporating this activity as part of their bedtime routine now gives them a chance to celebrate their victories, resolve any outstanding negative feelings from the day, and end on a high note by focusing on their desires. Hopefully, this feeds their overnight dreams with positive aspirations and grand adventures of the imagination.

Doing this exercise with my kids every day also gives me another opportunity to teach or reinforce positivity and lessons about choice. I help them process the events of the day and their feelings around them through the filter of their choices, the actions they took, and the outcomes of the events. This discussion provides them the building blocks for the life skills of problem-solving and dealing with their own emotions. Imagine how far ahead your kids will be if you teach them these skills at a young age.

I'm astonished at what I have learned through this exercise! It gives me tremendous insight into what's going on with each of my kids. It also gives me a chance to sincerely listen to them and hear about what is important to them in this phase of their life. I know those things will change as they grow, but this is an awesome way to stay connected and clued into what is going on in their heads. I listen to what they share, but even more importantly, I pay attention to how they share it. Are they coming from their head, "I think…" or their heart, "when this happened today, I felt…" Are they more kinesthetic, showing me by acting out their stories? This information is invaluable to understand how they relate to the world. If I pay attention and then use corresponding words and actions when I'm speaking to them, I'll be connecting with them on a much higher ban-width. I will be speaking their language and demonstrating my love for them in the frequency they resonate best with their language style. As a parent, wouldn't you love to be able to communicate this well with your children as they grow up?

So often, conversations between parents and kids sound like, "How was school today?" "Fine, what's for dinner?" … end of the conversation. There's no real exchange of information, no relationship building, no rapport, and no trust growing. If none of that exists for the basic stuff like the "How was school?"; what hope is there of any real dialogue when the questions are, "Are you in trouble?" or "Are you using drugs?" or "How can I help?"

Through local schools and charities, I do quite a bit of mentoring. I have used some of these communication techniques with my mentees. It's not surprising that they have built up emotional stone walls, given the obstacles and challenges facing some of them. It's often impossible to read their feelings, and I never know whether I'm making a difference. I'm always astonished when one of the kids shares something with me that lets me know, yes, I am getting through and helping them. Since the parents of these children usually come from similar family situations, they often demonstrate the same stoic exterior with their children, reinforcing these emotional guards.

Recently, I asked the kids in the program to write something they were thankful for on small gratitude cards. One of my mentees completely surprised me. He was brave enough to take a chance by letting his guard down. Unprompted, he wrote the nicest comments about me as his mentor and the positive effects on his life. When I read that card, I thought to myself. "Is this the same tough kid?" he's usually very reserved and difficult to read. He wants to shield himself from being hurt, so he comes across like a rock. Kids are incredible! Invest the time to build a rapport with them before asking them personal questions; if you do this, they will let you in and share their emotions. If you don't, you may never know what's going on inside or in their world.

After our kids are in bed, my wife, Jenny, and I can talk through our 3-2-1 for the day. We find it's a great way to share a recap of the day and its impact on each of us. It allows a glimpse into each other's experiences and provides room for praise, support, or calibration. When Jenny shares about her day, I might respond, "Oh, I didn't know you went through that today. Great job on how you handled that situation!" or "How can I help?"

A recent example was the day that one of her challenges was when Paisley threw a temper tantrum, as 4-year-olds do. My wife felt that it shouldn't have happened and that as a parent, she could have reacted differently to how our daughter behaved. We talked through strategies for managing the factors that triggered the episode and some thoughts on how to handle the behavior if it happens again.

Even though I was not there when the incident happened, talking through it together in a non-judgmental way allowed me to participate in the parenting process and support my partner-in-crime. We get a chance to align on everything from how the kids are doing to how much progress we are making on our family goals. My wife and I also enjoy creating and sharing our separate bucket lists for the upcoming month and year. We talk about our dreams and aspirations. We plan family trips and fun activities to do with the kids. Since we discuss everything, we stay connected, and we continue to grow as a couple through our constant communication.

With my businesses, I have a weekly meeting for each team where we do a modified version of the 3-2-1 Exercise. We go around the room and talk about goals and successes at the beginning of a meeting. We also do a "question of the day," such as "What is your favorite childhood memory?" The privilege of coming up with the questions gets passed around the room every week. It's a fun activity for the entire staff, and it's a different way to get to know each other. The goal of our meetings is to get the drama out and the good energy into the group. I will always take the time to plan these meetings and expect that my managers also outline what we need to discuss for the week. We brainstorm problem-solving, work through setting goals, and create 30-day action plans to achieve those goals.

As a leader at work, I am committed to cultivating a culture of open, honest, and drama-free communication.

In addition to the frequent manager meetings and the weekly staff meetings, I make a point regularly to connect with each staff member on an individual basis. When I hire someone onto one of my teams, they become a part of the "family." As a result, I want to get to know them as a person. I try to learn about who they are, what drives them, and how they like to be recognized. When I see them in the office and say hello or ask, "How's it going?" they know it is a sincere question, and feel how much I care. I am genuinely interested in their answer. I don't just ask and zone out or start talking over them. I actively listen and ask more questions. Caring and listening build trust, loyalty, and personal accountability.

The 3-2-1-communication technique is so powerful in building morale, heading off problems, and making people feel supported; it has become an integral part of our team meetings. Using this technique is like driving a car with a turbocharged engine; it's powerful, gives you a quick start to discussing successes and potential problems, and makes everyone feel like they're using a tool with a lot of muscle.

I am blessed, grateful, and I value the people in my life. I want to celebrate their successes and help them find opportunities to continue growing. As a positive person, I look for opportunities to praise a person's success at work publicly. I want our entire team to celebrate and feel genuine happiness when any of us does something good or has a success. For example, when an employee who is struggling with closing the sale on a particular product or upgrade finally sells it, I want to stand on the tallest building and tell the world that they did it! Recognition and celebration of the accomplishment give them confidence and momentum and bonds them more with the team. As leaders, we must be willing to acknowledge the good more often than the bad. Too frequently, leaders focus on the opportunities and teachable moments when something has gone wrong. Instead, lead from the perspective that every positive moment can also be a teachable moment, and those are how you nurture your mediocre or average employees into great ones. When communication comes from a genuine desire to help others, the results increase exponentially.

When there's an issue with an employee, or you need to investigate a situation, give your associates the courtesy and dignity of doing it privately. Always address it, don't ignore it. Problems do not go away on their own; they snowball into bigger problems if left unchecked. I sit down with each team member 1-on-1 and get to the root cause. I probe to discover what's going on, and hear their side of the story. During these 1-on-1's, my employees have on occasion revealed to me separate or deeper issues.

When your lines of communication are open, your team knows that even if they have done something wrong, you will give them the chance to explain. When you hear what they have done, you have to think, is it fixable? Is this a pattern? Is there more to the story? Another big takeaway from this lesson: address any issues before poor habits emerge. It should be obvious, if you've had this conversation with the same person several times, then there's a pattern here, and it's time to move on. I firmly believe that anybody who gets fired or laid off knows when it's coming because of clear communication and realistic expectations on both sides. I've left things on good terms and been able to maintain friendships with everyone who has worked for me.

Effective communication sometimes requires that you take time to gather your thoughts and consider your emotions. When life throws you a curve, anything from family drama to employee or customer confrontations is when the 24-hour rule comes into play. Simply put, you hit the "Pause Button" and give yourself 24-hours to respond. Sure some cases might require more immediate attention, and even fewer would be considered life-threatening situations requiring swift action. The majority of extraordinary things don't warrant your instant engagement. The 24-hour rule allows you time to reassess the information and process your emotions before taking any action. This break also allows others to reflect, take ownership, and offer any relevant facts and insight. In general, no matter what the event or bad news, take a 24-hour time out period. Inevitably you'll feel different 24 hours later.

Use this list as a way to create the 24-hour pause safely:
- Diffuse the situation
- Ensure everyone is safe

- If you're involved, remove yourself from the area (go outside for a walk, call a friend or coach, take a deep breath)
- Pull the employee or friend aside or send them home
- Ask a customer to leave
- Call security or police

Once you've taken the necessary time to reflect, gather more information, and consider the variables, you'll respond based on evidence and clear thinking rather than an impulsive reaction based on emotions. Follow this simple rule and avoid the regrets of rash assessments or actions made in the heat of the moment.

Successful, effective communication comes from active listening with genuine caring and leads to greater trust, understanding, and rapport between individuals and groups. Incorporating a technique like the 3-2-1 Exercise regularly into the culture can establish a healthy baseline for open dialogue. It can be easily adapted to fit most environments and participants at home or in the office. Trust, understanding, and rapport provide a platform on which more challenging conversations, including disciplinary ones, can be conducted with positive and productive outcomes. As a leader in business or at home, you must strive to create a setting that fosters quality communication.

Key Lesson Takeaways

Start today by taking 30 minutes to reflect on the stories in this lesson. Ask yourself the questions below and write down three ways to create lasting memories at home, at work, and in relationships.:

- ✓ What memories have shaped you?
- ✓ What kinds of memories am I creating with the people in my life?
- ✓ What mark will I leave on my family, business community, and the world?
- ✓ What memories do I have of others, that I keep alive?
- ✓ What will my legacy be?

Jenny's Advice

Listen with your whole heart to communicate effectively. It's the key to every type of relationship. When you need to discuss something difficult, start by saying something positive.

LESSON 5
Be the Best You- Strong Body, Strong Mind, Strong Heart

Photo by Brooke Lark on Unsplash

"Don't be the richest man in the graveyard."
~ Tony Robbins

When we talk about health, it's relevant to consider the wellbeing of our whole being, body-mind-spirit. In several places in this book, I discuss strategies for growing and maintaining your mind, so in this lesson, I want to focus on your body and spirit, more specifically, your heart and soul.

The purpose of this lesson is to help you understand your overall health, its effect on your business, family, and relationships, and how to make improvements that will last a lifetime.

A wide range of external and internal factors impact our health. Did you know that upwards of 90% of all visits to physicians are stress-related? If you didn't know that, you might be surprised to learn that all accumulated tension has a profound effect on our overall physical and mental health. Internally, everything from the health of your heart, diabetes, insomnia, headaches, and even cancers can be triggered or exacerbated by stress. Externally, it causes us to lose focus, miss details, amplify our risk of injury, and often drives up absenteeism. According to the American Psychological Association, 72% of people list money as the number one stressor.

There are some beneficial types of stress, such as weight-bearing pressure, to improve bone growth and density, or pregnancy, where the body endures significant physical changes, which results in the miracle of birth. The stress that I'm addressing here is an unhealthy strain. This type is detrimental to your whole health and causes dis-ease, interferes with growing and nurturing healthy relationships, and can be the reason for premature death.

Years ago, the American Entrepreneur, Jim Rohn, said, **"Take care of your body; it is the only place you have to live."**

This quote succinctly states how I think about taking care of my heart and overall health. I add the word "**Forev-er!**" to the end of his quote because it helps to remind me about the full meaning of the quote. We only get this one body, and it's our job to take care of it. Think about it, what's the point of everything else you do, if you're not around to enjoy it? It wasn't until I was married and had a family that I started to pay attention to my overall wellness. Perhaps that's because when we are younger, we think we're invincible. There's also a difference in how men and women handle stress. Women tend to identify and discuss their stressors while men will internalize. All that "keeping it to ourselves" makes us as men more susceptible to a depressed immune function and chronic illness. According to experts, improving and maintaining health and managing stress is the foundation for a long, quality life.

My mom passed away too young. No matter what age you are when you lose a parent, there will always be times that you miss them. While I know that she's still with me in spirit, I wish I could be sharing more of my success, joy, and life with her. She wasn't able to attend my wedding or to meet her grandchildren. I am determined to do whatever I need to so that I am around for my family, for many decades. There will always be factors that you can't control, so control the ones that you can.

I'm guessing that you already know that you should exercise, eat more vegetables and fruits and cut down on processed, fried and sugary foods. So, why is something so simple to understand so difficult for most people to achieve? In the Bending Time lesson, the segment about Determination is key to success here. You are in total control over how you choose to care for your health.

Success in this lesson requires two things we've already talked about, your Why and Determination. Wellness and heart health require you to do the work, you can't delegate them to someone else. That means you must be fully present and committed to the lifestyle changes required to take you from where you are to where you want to be.

You've heard the phrase, "Get up on the right side of the bed," I think every side is the right side if you have a positive attitude, plan to do something every day for your heart health, mind, and spirit. If you're looking to start a fitness routine, consider morning workouts, that's how I start my day. Did you know that your overall health has a direct effect on everyone who loves you? Being in the fitness industry for more than 13 years, I see firsthand the struggle of clients who don't have good health. I see it in the way their movement is restricted by pain or on the faces of their family members who want them to get healthier.

When I first wake up, I need to do cardio and get my heart pumping. Not because I want to have a six-pack or a beach body, I work out and particularly cardio exercise because I want to be able to play and keep up with my kids for as long as they enjoy my company. Be conscious of the choices you make today, tomorrow, and each day after. When it comes to fitness, you are in control!

Early morning exercise will help you start the day with more energy, focus, and optimism. Plus, after a morning workout, you're more likely to eat healthier and stay active throughout the day. After a workout, your metabolism increases for up to 24 hours. Which means your body is more efficient at calorie usage. Physical activity has other health benefits too. Science is unclear exactly how exercise improves the immune system, but they do know it works.

Exercise can help you manage your stress. Chronic stress is attributable to an increased incidence of cardiovascular disease, musculoskeletal issues, and psychological problems. Additionally, the risk of injury or illness increases, the longer the stress continues. Overworking can lead to insomnia, poor nutrition, weight gain, and elevated blood pressure. Jim Carey's quote provides a clear image of how everything is related to being healthy.

> *"I believe depression is legitimate. But I also believe that if you don't exercise, eat nutritious food, get sunlight, get enough sleep, consume positive material, surround yourself with support, then you aren't giving yourself a fighting chance."*
>
> ~ Jim Carey

Healthy eating can help in preventing so many chronic and lifestyle-related diseases, including obesity, heart disease, high blood pressure, and diabetes. About one in every ten Americans has diabetes. High blood sugar can trigger heart disease, vision loss, and kidney disease. Unfortunately, both childhood diabetes and obesity are on the rise in the US. The good news is that parents can take simple steps to reduce the odds of their children developing these medical conditions.

- Monitor or increase water intake
- Reduce the consumption of sugary drinks
- Increase fruits and vegetables
- Incorporate daily physical exercise

Talking about health with your kids can be one of the most important things you can teach your child. Show them the benefits of staying healthy, eating greens, and embracing fun outside activities. Fresh air is good for the soul, regardless of your age. Healthy eating habits and regular exercise are more likely to become a way of life for you if you learn these habits as children and see them reinforced in your role models.

My wife was a Physical Education teacher for five years, and I have been a gym owner for 14 years, so we definitely want our kids to understand the importance of health. We have gotten our kids involved in a variety of sports. We want them to try all activities, then decide which ones they like best. We're leaving the choice entirely up to them to make. We ride bikes, hike, run, workout in our basement gym, and play sports in our backyard on average every other day. It's our priority to get outside in the fresh air. We shoot for three hours of exercise per week for our children. Depending on your kids' age, you should adjust the frequency, duration, and types of activities.

In 2017, I focused on my health by making significant changes. For starters, I gave up all carbs, beer, and sugar for the entire year. I wouldn't allow myself to cheat because I know myself well enough to know that even one exception would open the flood gates and soon I would be back to square one. I admit that I have an addictive personality and, being a fan of extremes, can manifest as either a blessing or a curse. Knowing this, I was able to leverage it to work in my favor. I had to set serious boundaries, create rules, and promise myself that I would not break them. Like other times in my life, I tapped into my willpower to help me attain a stronger heart and better health. When you want something badly enough, and have a big enough "why you want it," you too can use grit and determination to accomplish your goal. That's right, the very same grit and determination we discussed in Chapter 3, Bending Time. Do you see how the lessons I am teaching you in this book overlap and can assist you in all phases of your life?

So how did I do it? Well, my rules were simple:

DO Eat:
- Natural foods from the earth
- Fruit and vegetables
- Lots of protein (meat, fish, chicken, shakes, etc)

DO NOT Eat:
- Processed Foods
- Bread, tortillas
- Desert (including birthday cake)
- Beer (even during a football game)

Honestly, I was never a sweets person, but tortillas and beer were a big deal to me. I said I like extremes, and maybe this seems extreme to you, but it worked for me. To decide what's best for you:
- Get clear on your Why
- Be honest with yourself

- Set specific goals
- Create a plan
- Take Action - grab this by the horns and tackle it
- Don't Stop

Are you curious about my results? I found a new balance in my life. I shed 30 pounds, and to this day, I still feel better than I've ever felt. It requires less effort for me to keep up with my young kids. The most important outcome was that I proved to myself that I could be 100% true to the plan I created to improve my health. I kept reminding myself of my big Why, my ultimate goal; to be there for my kids later in life and be the best dad I can be. I would have failed without knowing my why and digging deep to access my determination. Today, I use the "all things in moderation" overall approach to eating.

Do:

- Put greens in your mouth as much as possible
- Be aware of calories in and calories out
- Watch what you consume
- It's a lifestyle, NOT a diet
- Enjoy your favorite meal, just make up for it in the next few meals

Do Not:

- Overeat or gorge. STOP when you are full. Just like a baby, when they are full, they stop. Somewhere as adults, we lose this concept and eat for enjoyment.

- Eat Carbs with every meal
- Eat Fast food daily for convenience

If you want to improve your heart health and wellness, follow my plan to succeed. You don't have to be as extreme as I am, you can start in whatever way is best for you. Once you create your plan of how you will achieve health, don't abandon it on a whim because it gets hard, or your friends are over watching the big game, and you want to drink or eat things on your avoid list. Keep revisiting your why, focus on your goals, and use your plan to succeed.

As I've previously mentioned, balance is a state of being that requires awareness. Awareness provides you with a panoramic view of what you're consistently doing, allowing for more streamlined adjustments to your plans. One overriding goal here to keep in mind is to strive for balance in all things. Balance is the pathway to better ease in your life and improved health. Perfection is a path to dis-ease and stress. Always check with your medical advisor before beginning any new physical activity or implementing dietary changes.

There's one more bonus that I haven't told you about; I found a love for waking up early! That one surprised me. When I first met my wife, Jenny, I was a night owl, up until midnight or 1:00 am, and she always wanted to get up by 7 or 8 in the morning. I would delay getting up and stay in bed as late as possible, often only minutes before I had to go to work. In those days, I was barely on time, but never late! Back then, I was unaware of how being a night owl and a last-minute to work guy, created totally avoidable stressors. Now, all that has changed for me. Something happens when you change your sleep habits and create a morning plan where time is on your side. Your heart and soul thrive in your new regiment. It really works for me. Now, I'm up every morning around 4:30 and pumped to dive into my day. I have so much more energy, and I am positive about getting up early because of what I can accomplish. I discuss this concept of getting up early, in greater detail, in the Chapter on BENDing Time.

There is no free lunch when it comes to wellness; you physically have to do the work. You cannot get in shape by merely watching a YouTube video of someone running or eating right. YOU and only you have to put in the work to attain the results. As we say in the gym business, you can never outrun a bad diet.

It may seem like I have a lot of "rules" around things I do, but I also have three things that I will never do.

- I don't gamble.
- I don't do drugs.
- I don't play video games.

That may sound weird, and I am not placing a value judgment on those activities specifically. Still, I know that those activities with my addictive personality and fierce competitiveness would be catastrophic in my life.

The way that I work, if I were to do these things, I would have to be the best at them. I would do them so much to prove that I get more enjoyment out of them and that I'm the best, in fact, better than anyone else that's ever done gambling/drugs/games. I'd be so good at it, but I'd be on the streets and homeless or dead. I think it would be too easy for me to lose track of time, money, and eventually myself. Therefore, I won't start down any one of these roads. So I just don't.

When you're looking at your overall health, determine if you have an addictive personality, if so, decide where you need some, "I will never …" guidelines for yourself.

Know where you're starting from on your heart health/whole health journey.

- Get a physical medical
- Track your numbers (starting point --> goals)
- Identify activities you like or want to try
- Determine if you need to change your eating or sleeping habits
- Start with incremental changes
- Create a plan that's not overwhelming but gets you to your goals
- Be Bold in your goals but not crazy
- Start where it makes sense for you
- Have an accountability partner
- It's more than just physical health

The most important thing is to figure out what works for you and COMMIT to it! Stick with whatever plan you choose. Your health is worth it. You can also use technology with heart rate monitors such as Fitbit, Myzone, or Apple watch to track your progress. Today's cell phones also provide reasonably accurate results. Use that data to your advantage. Just be 1% better every day! Just 1%

In addition to your physical health, it's also essential to take care of your mental, emotional, and spiritual health. You need some "me" time for yourself and "we" time for you and your spouse or partner. Parents especially need to carve out some downtime; otherwise, it's all too easy to lose yourself. Failing to focus on you as individuals and as a couple can lead to miscommunications or physical and emotional distance. Ideally, you should want to be the couple that wants to do things together, who talks and laughs with each other rather than the couples who go through the motions or are two ships passing each other and living separate lives.

Your partner is the most significant and influential adult in your life; it's your job to maintain a solid foundation.

I feel like the luckiest man in the world to have found my soulmate.

But let's face it, even a soulmate requires work. My relationship isn't a chore, it's something that I want to nurture and grow. Our relationship is worth the effort we put into caring for it. Treating your senses to some gentleness now and then can be very therapeutic and beneficial to your partnership. Some easy and fun ways to engage with each other include taking a bubble bath and light some candles or scheduling a massage. Read, seek joy in life, and schedule time to reset, rest, and relax together.

Take care of your relationship, body, mind, and spirit. You both deserve and probably need a date night. Have a glass of wine together. Sit by a fire and talk. Strengthen your connections. I'm big on communication, and the result of consistent, high-quality dialogue, is getting closer to the people in your life. If this all sounds awkward for you or if you and your spouse have drifted, you need to start connecting now, not tomorrow, or next weekend, but immediately. Keep working at it, taking small steps together until the awkwardness evaporates, and you notice that you look forward to this part of your day.

Align with your spouse, and you will naturally find that you're engaging differently and more authentically with everyone else in your life. While all the people in your life will benefit from your consistent and caring communication, you'll discover that the benefits you receive are wide-ranging. Any internal burdens or stress that you carry should lighten because you are opening up to others just as they are with you. Sharing and caring is one way to release the pressure valve.

I also find it refreshing to meditate, pray, go for a hike, or meet up with friends. Have you ever noticed that afterward, you feel much more like yourself? That's because these activities deliver benefits to the wellbeing of your body, mind, and spirit. Regularly incorporating these types of healthy activities balance out the negative impacts of tension and reduce the detrimental hormones released from stress. It's important to integrate activities that feed your heart and soul if you want to live a long and happy life.

Water, sleep, and touch all play critical roles in heart health and whole health. I set my intention to drink a lot of water, get plenty of good quality sleep, and get or give eight hugs a day. Family therapist, Virginia Satir, believes we need eight hugs a day to maintain optimal health. Science has shown hugs reduce stress, protect you against illness, boost heart health, make you happier, overcome fears, help reduce pain, and help you communicate with others.

Pre-pandemic, my advice would have been, if you're not a hugger, then start by hugging your children, your spouse, parents, and closest friends. Not those "bro-hug" kinds of hugs, where you come in lock hands for a moment, give a quick pat on the back and release. Ideally, to give and receive the benefits of hugging, give a hug with intention, and linger for a moment so both people can truly feel the benefit. With the pandemic, we have to balance physical distancing for everyone's safety with the health benefits of hugging. If you don't live alone, start hugging those with whom you're living. If you live alone, connect in ways that allow you to give and receive virtual hugs such as meditation, video chats with your loved ones, or even sending e-cards or emails to convey your intention of hugging. Everything in this world right now is an experiment on how to be creative and still get what we need. You are not alone, ask for, and create what you need.

When we are at our finest or making improvements that will take us on a path toward our best self, our business, relationships, and personal side all benefit in both expected and unexpected ways.

- Increased energy
- Positive attitude
- Eating well
- Exercising
- Improved Sex Life
- Surrounded by people who care about each other
- Better quality sleep
- Caring for Body/Mind/Spirit
- Family First (home and work)
- Deep Connections
- Improved Relationships
- Stronger sense of direction
- Ability to plan and follow through
- Dedication
- Creative Problem Solving

It's equally important to me that my team members are healthy and happy. I encourage self-care, fitness, and fun across all of my businesses in a variety of ways. Every employee receives a free membership to my gym. I like training with my team, I am always learning something new. I'm right there alongside them participating in a variety of classes. It's some of what makes our bond strong. Your team knows when you care about them, and my team knows they are family. In turn, this bond creates a healthy business.

We even started a United Way/ Snap Fitness 4th of July 5K for our community. This event began as a fun way to get people out, move their bodies, and give back to our community. Fourteen years later, our 5K is the second largest in southern Colorado. We draw 500-1,000 participants to the event. To this day, our teams feel a significant level of energy and excitement preparing for and participating in this event. It's more than a 5K; it's a family-run that encourages all aspects of health, and people amp up the fun by wearing patriotic theme costumes. I'm always surprised at how many people tell me this was their first 5k and that it ignited their journey to running, health, or racing. For me, that is Mission Accomplished! As you know from the Bending time lesson, I love a good triple dip. At this event, we raise money for a fantastic organization, highlight the benefits of health, and increase visibility for our businesses.

Use this lesson to map out where you are and how you want to upgrade your life. Only you can level up your own life. You are the determining factor, therefore, create your own rules and use any of mine to assist.

Ask yourself:

- Am I feeding myself the fuel that feeds my brain?
- Am I taking care of my heart, mind, and spirit?
- How can I create more balance?
- Who do I know that can hold me accountable?
- Am I doing all that I can?
- Do I make my family and employees feel special?
- Do I express my gratitude?
- Do I share my concerns with someone who can help relieve my pressures?
- Am I giving my partner everything I've got?
- Am I truly giving my kids what they need?
- Am I committing myself 100% to success in my business
- Am I living my best life?

Too many people suffer from lifestyle-related diseases and chronic conditions that lead to an early death. Most people won't take the time to change their role in these statistics. So much of health is controllable; we can control our stress, heart, and mind.

Don't become a statistic! Remove yourself from the equation of dis-ease. Start today, make some changes, and build upon those changes until you get to where you want to be. If you can control it, why wouldn't you'? DO IT NOW!

Do your part to live a long healthy life. You, your family, and employees deserve your best!

Key Lesson Takeaways

- ✓ Use the questions listed above to identify areas of your overall health in which you are doing well and those that are out of balance
- ✓ Make a plan to strengthen the parts that are working well and address those that are not
- ✓ Over the next 30-days, keep a journal or log of your health-related activities and note your progress
- ✓ Check-in with your accountability coach weekly to stay on course. If you don't have an accountability coach, GET ONE Today!
- ✓ Keep your body in motion

Jenny's Advice

To live a healthy lifestyle, I'm telling you that it's ok to put yourself first. As a past Physical Education teacher, I know this to be true. It's never too late! I'm proud of my mother, who we call Mother Goose. She took charge of her health and can now keep up with her grandchildren.

LESSON 6
Adapt and Transform

> *"The measure of intelligence is the ability to change."*
>
> ~ Albert Einstein

Are you a Sports Authority or a Garmin?

Have you noticed we live in a world where everything seems to be changing every minute? Adapting to the rapidly changing world we live in is crucial for survival and fundamental for achieving great success. Both as a Dad and an entrepreneur, being able to "read the room" and adjust to new or emerging variations is essential. Each of your team members and children may require a slightly different delivery of the same message. As the father of two young boys and a little girl, I can attest that not much works the same for each kid. I always have to think on my feet. When I talk about 'challenges', please don't mistake it for "difficult parenting" because, as a parent, you will have your obstacles, and that's just life. The ability to get through them a little wiser and more capable is the mark of growth and good parenting. Apply these learnings to your business. About the time you think you understand your kids, they grow, and just when you feel you have your employees motivated and moving forward, something shifts for them too. Some people are driven by financial rewards, some by pride or the title; others are just competitive by nature. Understanding people's Why helps you tailor your message to what makes them tick. So you need to have the ability to adapt while always staying positive. Each new circumstance that arises requires that you transform the skills or knowledge you have gained from previous experiences to suit this new one.

In the various roles of my life, I work with people from a wide range of diverse backgrounds. Each individual has a unique personality and passion. Sometimes I have to adapt my message, communication style, listening, and questions. To understand someone else, you need to spend the time getting to know them, recognize what's important to them, and value their perspective and personal history. When you take the time to do that, your interactions transform into more meaningful connections.

I never thought about how pet peeves can impact relationships and perception. Do you have any pet peeves that are affecting your relationships or business? Think about that for a moment. The first time I thought about it was when my oldest son, Parker, was still a toddler. He loved wearing cowboy boots and shorts. This combination used to drive me crazy! It took me shifting my perspective to realize the moment was about Parker, not about me. His outfit was not a safety or core value issue. It was merely an expression of his free will to make choices. I didn't want to crush that spirit, and I had more important lessons to teach him. My priority was ensuring he was growing up as a great person, treating people, especially his family, with love, respect, and integrity. So I thought, "Parker, wear those damn boots with shorts if that's what you want to do! You do you!" As a parent, we need to allow our children to be themselves. The same is true in no small measure for your staff in the work environment.

They say that kids learn by example. I think that's true for kids, adults, employees, and employers. I have witnessed in action, one of my favorite quotes from a friend, mentor, and former colleague Bruce Damm.

> "More is caught than taught."

As my son, Parker, gets older and smarter, we have noticed that he hears everything, and by everything I mean EVERYTHING! Even when he was only three years old, we noticed he started picking up on so much more in his environment. Parker became aware of what and how Jenny and I were doing or saying in every situation. He also noticed, processed, and began to question the actions of everyone around him. He saw patterns of behavior and places of disconnect. We had to seriously consider this in everything we did and didn't do or say in front of him, from parenting disagreements to how we interacted with other people. Everything was being observed and absorbed into the eyes and ears of our watchful Parker. Jenny's advice is to remember that your kids, just like ours, are sponges, soaking in everything you do and say. So make the most of it and teach them valuable life skills along the way. They will do as you do, from eating healthy, exercising, cleaning, to being kind and generous.

Learning through seeing is as prevalent in the business world as in the parenting world. If children are catching everything at the age of three, imagine how much an adult can pick up simply through casual observation. It is imperative that what you are modeling is demonstrating the way you want your employees to act. They watch how you approach customers, treat vendors, manage your time, solve problems, and handle stress. In every interaction with customers, my goal is to make sure that when they leave, they say, "Wow, that was an awesome experience" I want my team to follow my lead and provide that same level of service. Your team notices if you are "walking the walk or just talking the talk." It's also good practice that they see you having fun and can join you.

If I am going to expect my kids and my staff to say please, thank you, and open doors for others, because I believe in common courtesy, then I better be saying and doing those things consistently myself. If I don't say thank you every time I ask them for something, why would I expect them to do it? *"More is caught than taught."* If you don't lead by example, your kids and your staff will call you on it by saying, "But you didn't do it, Dad/Matt, so why do I have to? "You're right; how can I expect you to do that if I'm not doing it myself?" At Disney, even the top executives pick up trash in the park.

Hold yourself accountable because everyone deserves that. They might not always come out and tell you right away, but they're watching, and they remember more than you think. I have many coaches in my life to help me grow, challenge me, and hold me accountable for the goals I set. They help me to be much more responsive and even proactive. With the big picture in mind and clear goals, I can quickly pivot my company's direction or my family's. Personal accountability and clear, timely communication improve your relationships, business, friendships, and family. Harmony in all aspects of your life will create a sense of inner peace and allow you to experience more fluid adaptability. You will feel joy with who you are and who you are becoming.

Have you ever resisted adapting to necessary changes at home or business? How do you help your family and employees accept and embrace change?

On the business side of my life, I'm choosing to make a significant change of direction. Since I opened my mattress business, I've dreamt of building brick and mortar locations nationwide. I envisioned stores all over the country that began here in my beautiful Pueblo, Colorado. That idea had to change when a 6-month expansion project for Snap Fitness took over two years. Learning this about construction timelines, I realized I couldn't accept the math. If one project takes two years, and I plan to build as many locations as possible over the next ten years, then at that rate, I could only have five new brick and mortar stores. That was nowhere near fast enough for the pace I want to achieve. I needed to adapt my methods. I briefly considered investors to move more quickly. I searched for the best options to go as big as I could in the shortest amount of time, so I could ultimately spend more time with my family.

At this moment, I am reaching out to experts who have gone nationwide with their companies to learn more about how they reached that next level. I am considering franchising our model, creating more entrepreneurs, selling online to a broader audience, and buying existing buildings and retrofitting them instead of new construction.

Sometimes you switch direction in business not because your vision has changed but because the market has and what you are currently doing is no longer working well or losing money. If you have owned a business, you have lost money in a week, a month, or even a year. Fluctuations in income come with the territory in almost any industry. The ability to recognize when it's more than a blip and make timely course corrections to a formula that's no longer working is essential to business growth and longevity.

I once owned a tuxedo business called Mister Penguin Tuxedos. The store had been around for 30 years in our community. The business model for the company's entire history was simple; make a lot of money during prom and wedding season and lose money for the rest of the year. Yes, you read that right. They planned to lose money for the rest of the year! This seasonal business plan to cover payroll for more than four months with no business coming in the doors did not make any sense to me. When we bought the company, one of my best friends and business partner, Adam Sanchez, and I agreed to modify the plan.

We asked ourselves, "What is a complementary business that our current customer base would support?" Quality dresses and suits made sense to me. We found a reliable vendor and began perfecting the suit business. It didn't cost much more than adding a few new displays and the time it took to learn about our new products. By simply adding a new product line, a business model that had stagnated over the 30 years was updated and expanded. Instead of being a seasonal tuxedo shop that was barely staying afloat in the off-season, we morphed it into a suit sales business that rented tuxedos as a sideline. Now, Mister Penguin is profitable all year long.

Adapt and Transform

Here are two recent examples of major companies, brands that you should recognize, which faced market shifts that demanded they adapt or perish.

First, there's Sports Authority, a Denver, Colorado-based, sporting goods retailer. At their peak, they were number one in the nation with more than 450 locations across the country. From all appearances, they positioned themselves to succeed for years to come. They even owned the naming rights to the Denver Broncos Stadium when the Broncos were riding high with winning seasons and two trips to the Super Bowl. Suddenly, they were facing significant issues that called for drastic changes. Sports Authority didn't face just one problem; they had to overcome a list of obstacles:

- Flatlined revenue growth
- Overleveraged by updates to brick and mortar stores
- Ill-equipped for the rapid growth of online shopping (e-commerce in general and Amazon.com in particular)
- Growing market share by a direct competitor, Dick's Sporting Goods
- Behind-the-times fashion product lines
- Lack of a private label brand
- Uninformed and under enthusiastic sales team
- Mediocre store environment

Unfortunately for Sports Authority, they did not respond in time, or with drastic enough measures to save the retail giant. Most managers, including a close relative of mine, were taken by surprise. The company appeared to be charging ahead; business as usual as if nothing was wrong, wasn't anyone looking at the profit and loss statements or the quarterly projections? It's hard to say whether it was the lack of leadership, financial burdens, or the poor quality of shopping experience that prevented them from pivoting when the market changed. The apparent inability to adapt and transform resulted in Chapter 11 Bankruptcy, liquidation of merchandise, dismissal of all 14,000 employees, and total closure of all stores.

Then there is Garmin, a global company, headquartered in Kansas City, Kansas, with select retail locations. They specialize in Global Positioning System (GPS) navigation and wearable technology for automotive, aviation, marine, outdoor, and fitness applications. I still remember my first Garmin. I was a massive fan because, before smartphones, I was always getting lost! Until I got a Garmin, I would frequently have to make about 5 U-turns to find my destination. In 2007, Garmin was the industry leader in GPS systems for cars, bringing in $2.5 billion in sales, representing three-quarters of its annual revenue. Enter, Apple iPhone with integrated Google Maps making the Garmin device almost obsolete. Losing their auto market share all but crippled the company. They had to find a new way to compete or be eliminated.

Fortunately for Garmin, the co-founders believed in the principle of doing everything in-house. From marketing to manufacturing, they were in total control of their direction and timing. Not being at the mercy of vendor or partner schedules enabled them to respond immediately. With the advances in technology, Garmin saw an opportunity in the wearable market. They shifted their focus from automotive to wearable devices and carved out a niche. They didn't try to sell to everyone; they focused on their die-hard customer base, the avid cyclist, runners, triathletes, swimmers, golfers, hikers, and outdoor enthusiasts. They offered high quality, technologically advanced, reliable equipment. Garmin products are sold through e-commerce and in experience-based retail outlets where their brand-loyal customers like to shop.

Garmin did it right:
- Analyzed the trends
- Found an untapped market/technology
- Re-tooled their operation
- Focused on a particular niche
- Provided quality and reliability
- Created small retail footprints tailored to their customer base
- Engaging online presence
- User-friendly e-commerce
- Introduced the Garmin App store allowing third-party programmers to create Apps that are compatible with Garmin products

When Garmin eventually decided to expand into the entry-level fitness tracker market, they did so with a specific purpose. They didn't just throw spaghetti at the wall, waiting to see what stuck. They intended to introduce the product line to a new segment of customers and gradually move them up the value ladder to their higher-priced products. Garmin's market value has grown steadily over the past five years.

> *"Make yourself obsolete or someone else will."*
> ~ Thom Shearer

On face value, you can take this quote to mean that if you are not already the best in your industry and continually striving to be better, then a competitor will come along and outdo you, making you obsolete. You may also embrace this message beyond the apparent surface-level application. Internally, you can look at it personally and understand that the advice is always to reinvent and upgrade you. Externally, you can interpret this idea to mean that if you innovate a new concept or practice that is superior or more efficient than the current standard, the industry will change. The reality of evolution is that it will eventually change anyway. If you are proactive and creative enough, you might be at the leading edge of that transformation. Change is the only constant. Don't be left behind.

I'm continually evolving myself and my businesses. I enlarged Snap Fitness three times, and every year upgraded and purchased new equipment. I increased the size of the spa three times. I bought all new equipment and new vans for the Carpet business. Each time I upgrade or grow in the market, I make myself and the company a little stronger. These improvements probably stopped potential competitors from entering the market or expanding. Be the strongest competitor in your market, so that nobody wants to compete against you.

During the completion of the Snap Fitness construction, the commercial space next door went up for sale. I knew if there were ever a time to get back into the mattress business, it would be right then. Making that happen at the same time took some creative out-of-the-box financing. The bank hadn't even completed funding the last project yet. But, I trusted my gut and jumped on the opportunity.

While in quarantine and writing parts of this book, I started a marketing company. Based on the changes in consumer behavior, I could see the direction the market was going, and I decided to adapt to be out in front. The creativity, energy, fun, and innovation that comes out of this amazing group daily has opened my eyes to so many future possibilities. If you have an idea, don't wait, figure out how to make it happen and go for it!

If you've ever heard of the 1% rule or the 80/20 principle, then you understand that it doesn't take a huge difference to beat out your competition and control the majority of the resources. It requires having a slight advantage over them day after day. When resources are limited, as in nature, sunlight, water, and soil nutrients, the plant that can grow just a little faster or taller can edge out the plant next to it and begin to take more resources. Each day that it consumes more sun, water, and nutrition, it can grow even more than the day before and more than the neighboring plant. Eventually, it will completely overshadow the smaller, weaker plant and control most or all of the resources. The same is true in business and life. If you can stay just a little bit ahead of everyone else, you will thrive and reap the most abundant rewards.

Done correctly, making yourself obsolete in one area frees you up to be more relevant in another. As a parent, this might mean that once your child masters feeding himself, you next teach him to get his cereal and eventually to cook. In business, establish standard operating procedures for routine tasks, and create systems to train your team to handle the essential duties of running the company in its current capacity. Then, the progression is to teach them to grow it to the next level.

As I have discussed throughout this book, you should be obsessed with growth in all areas of your life personally and in business. Technology advances exponentially every year, so it may not be the best use of time and resources to try to keep up with every new gadget. Stay current enough to utilize the most effective or efficient tools for the job. Another facet of my continually evolving life is the systems that I employ in my businesses and my home. Whether it's training my team to train their replacement or showing my oldest son how to tie his shoes and having him teach his sister, planned obsolescence equals progress.

I'm sure you have heard the expression, "Knowledge is power", I am an absolute believer! Between Audible and Podcasts, I am always learning through listening. Steadily expanding my information library keeps my brain actively compiling data and feeding new ideas. Anytime you think about something new you want to try, you can quickly immerse yourself in the relevant views on the subject by tuning in to a book or podcast. Alternatively, you can seek an expert in the field and find a way to absorb what they have mastered. What's more important than how you gain knowledge, is how you use it!

Another part of yourself that warrants elevation is your mindset. I recommend doing an honest assessment of your attitude and convictions through self-reflection, personal observation, and candid feedback from someone close to you, a spouse, partner, or coach. It's helpful to get an accurate picture of how you respond to various challenges throughout your daily life to ensure you are as positive, organized, and clear as you think you are. Much like performing routine maintenance on your car or spring-cleaning around the house, you need to assess the areas of yourself that require additional development. By keeping your "personal" house in order, you create an opportunity to celebrate your progress and identify the aspects that need more attention.

It's a substantial competitive advantage to think big picture and long term, rather than trying to fix the short-term problems and staying small-minded. Sometimes those problems are just small potatoes. Stay focused on the broader vision and delegate the more immediate incidentals to your team. Treat every day as a new day, and keep working toward tomorrow's win!

> *"Adapt or die!"*
> ~ Charles Darwin

Adapt and Transform

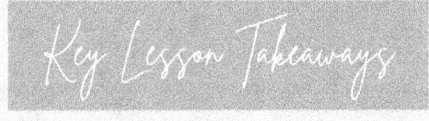

Key Lesson Takeaways

- ✓ Take a closer look at your business and family
- ✓ Identify outdated or obsolete mindsets, methods, and approaches
- ✓ Tune-Up or upgrade those areas
- ✓ Observe the results over the next 30, 60, and 90 days
- ✓ Research where you market or industry is headed and get ahead of it
- ✓ Discover what's next for your kids and get better at that
- ✓ Dream bigger
- ✓ Learn the language and the Why for each of your family members and coworkers

Jenny's Advice

I love to learn new things, but I'm also a creature of habit. Experiences are what allows us to grow. Every day something new is happening, and you get the opportunity to learn and grow. The more you know and the more open you are to experiences and new things, the more alive you feel.

LESSON 7

Who's on your Bus? Culture, Systems, And People

Photo by Ash Gerlach

Culture - it's more than yogurt!

When it comes to having the right people in your life, building your business, or developing your family, it all hinges on the culture you establish and the systems you create. When the culture makes people feel safe, respected, and valued, and the systems provide support, growth, and fun, they enjoy being there and are far more likely to be loyal and engaged.

At home, we balance creating a culture that makes plenty of room for fun and love with a system that gives enough structure to teach personal responsibility and mutual respect. Although the specifics will evolve as your kids grow up, the core values you instill in them at a young age should carry through their lifetime. Often, I hear parents who struggle to get their teenagers to pick up their rooms or do homework. These struggles are unfortunate and unnecessary. When they were young, we started training positive behaviors with our children by making games or competitions out of doing chores. This approach showed them how taking care of their toys and clothes and being mindful of how they treat other people's belongings can be fun and rewarding. You must reinforce these lessons by setting a good example of how you manage personal items. Adding the element of fun to any activity is a great way to anchor the learning. Be creative, and you can make a game out of any chore from putting away the dishes to brushing their teeth.

Jenny is amazing at creating a structure for the kids and presenting the rationale in a way they comprehend. If you're going to play with one toy or game, then the last one you had out had better be cleaned up and put away first. It's never too early to teach the basics of organization and tidiness. That's just one example of the rules that we have implemented. Right now, the two oldest are at an age where they are learning chores and responsibilities. One might set the table, and the other clears the table and does all the dishes. Each week, as they grasp a new task, we give them another to keep them stimulated and to feel a sense of pride in their growth. In a way, it says to them that you guys are old enough now to do this task, soon you can learn how to do the next thing. While teaching them valuable lessons and life skills, it also allows my wife and me to be smarter with our time. The kids do the majority of the picking-up throughout the day instead of us spending hours straightening up the house after they go to bed. It only takes a minute after each event or activity to clean it up before moving on to the next one. It just makes sense, and there is infinitely less stress this way!

Using this simple rule is implementing a system and bending time, both of which result in additional quality time spent together as a family. If your kids are teenagers, maybe you can teach them how to do the laundry, fold it, and put it away. Your children will develop a strong sense of integrity, inclusion, and pride in the home and the family unit. This experience builds a solid foundation and sets them on the path to being good people who contribute to society.

Disciplining your children is another area where culture and systems can genuinely make a difference. A s parents, we try to guide our children safely through the adventures of life. Part of growing up is that kids will periodically make mistakes or poor decisions. When those occasions happen, Jenny and I address them with the same approach as any other interactions, with love and open communication. We do not yell at or belittle our children; instead, we ask questions and give them a chance to explain themselves. After listening to their thought process and feelings about what they did, we help them see where they may have gone wrong in their assumptions or decision-making process. We share concerns about their choices or behaviors and the resulting impacts on them and the family. We clear up any misunderstanding about the expectations going forward. I believe it's also essential to get an acknowledgment of understanding and a commitment at the end of any disciplinary conversation with your children. You want to be sure they comprehend the core issues, take responsibility for their actions, and promise to make a better choice next time.

We have recently introduced the concept of allowance to our two oldest children. It provides an additional reward and recognition system for good behavior and completing chores or tasks. It also serves as a way to teach or reinforce the consequences of their actions. We have set up a simple system whereby they start each day with a certain amount that they can earn by following the rules and doing chores throughout that day. If, however, they misbehave or fail to do a task when asked, they can lose all or part of the day's allocated amount. Our disciplinary conversations now include a statement that says, "now that we have talked about this situation and you understand why you are not supposed to do X if you do it again, you will lose a $1 from that day's allowance." Spelling it out in this way makes the consequence more immediate and tangible.

Another exciting aspect of the allowance program is that it enables us to teach them about money and their relationship to it. Our approach has fostered a healthy competition between the two kids to see if they can earn the maximum available for the week. On Fridays, we sit down with them on Amazon and let them spend what they made during the week or hold onto it until they have saved up enough for a more expensive item. If we weren't in lockdown because of the pandemic, we would shop in our local stores. I absolutely believe in supporting local businesses and for the kids, walking through the store, and seeing the toys and games to choose from is a far richer experience than shopping online. The coolest part for me is that they often select projects like Legos or wooden building sets for their toy. It's a win/win because I get to spend more bonding time with them while we work together to construct the set. Let's be honest, we all like to be a big kid and play with Legos occasionally. Online shopping deliveries are not arriving as quickly as usual, due to the pandemic, so, the kids experience delayed gratification, which is another excellent lesson.

As our kids have gotten old enough, we have started to include them in some planning and decision-making processes around the family schedule. We try to take some of their wishes into consideration, but it's also our role as parents to set realistic expectations. I was driving the kids home from school one day before the pandemic, and I asked them what they wanted to do for our evening playtime. They are 4 and 5 years old, so they could come up with 100 things to do, including going to the park, building sandcastles, playing tag, hide-n-seek, checkers, frisbee, and soccer. I explained that we did not have time to do everything on their list in only one day, so they needed to prioritize or pick the top three choices, and put them in order on how we would do them. I feel it's valuable to get them talking about what they want and how to make it happen. Understanding the concept of prioritizing is also a beneficial life skill.

Do you struggle with the ability to rank assignments? Effective prioritization requires practice to develop mastery. Are you someone who struggles or stresses over how to set proper order accurately? Imagine the time saved and reduced stress if you had learned this skill as a child? I have decided to give my kids a head start in life and teach them this aptitude now. As they grow and the demands of school, sports, and jobs compete for their attention, this know-how will give them an advantage.

In my philosophy of "Family First," siblings are friends. We have created the family culture that the children are best friends, setting the expectation that they need to be there for each other. I feel that it is significant to instill a sense of connection and commitment to last their lifetime. They genuinely love and care for one another. They protect and stand up for each other. I want them to live, love, and enjoy playing together, creating a history of fun, loving memories with no regrets. You probably train your employees and roll play with them, putting significant effort into helping them build their skills. Do you do the same for your family? If the kids mistreat or are unkind to each other, have a conversation to correct the behavior, discipline them if need be, then have them apologize to each other, and hug it out. Healing and growth naturally happen when we work through it together.

At their ages of 4 and 5, the conflicts are small and don't last long but as a parent, I see the most significant piece of those spats is for them to recognize the behavior and practice the tools of reconciliation. For example, sometimes Parker, my oldest son, has another boy, a friend from the neighborhood over to play. Paisley can quickly feel left out because of the dynamics of two boys. This same thing goes when Paisley is with her girlfriends.

When disagreements or hurt feelings happen, as they can with any siblings, we go through these simple steps to resolve the issue, forgive and move forward together stronger.

1. We sit the kids down, help them understand how they are treating their best friend and sibling.
2. Get them to agree on a solution, apologize to each other, and admit where they may have been wrong.
3. Hug it out. Always end an argument with a hug. To me, it brings it all full circle and ends on a high note. It is not always easy after a fight, but it is 100% necessary, and they will see the value.

In several places in this book, I have mentioned how important it is 'to be present' and in the moment with the people whom you are with and whatever you are doing. It bears repeating here. There is nothing worse than a family sitting down to a meal around the table but not truly being together. It happens when they are all on their phones or engaged in some other solo activity, and nobody is making any progress on connecting to the family or building relationships.

This quarantine is a prime example. Depending on how long this lasts, families will spend 30, 60, or 90 days held-up in their houses together, and some will be essentially unchanged in their relationships or even worse off than when it started. Others, like my family, are treating this time isolating together as a gift. We are spending quality time together, learning about each other, instilling new healthy habits, playing games, reading, developing a more in-depth understanding, and a stronger bond. Making progress as a family unit has been a positive outcome of the pandemic shutdown. Has the pandemic shutdown strengthened your family bonds? If not, ask yourself what you can do to shift the dynamics. Initiate activities with your family that require interaction. Give each family member a turn in choosing the game or event to do together. Rotating responsibilities is fun and builds confidence that you trust each other.

As Dads, the connections we have with our kids can show up in the most surprising ways. On a family trip to Las Vegas, the hotel pool had a water slide. Imagine those famous Vegas water slides. They're heart-stoppingly impressive and exciting, and to a five-year-old, it becomes the only adventure they've ever wanted. Parker desperately wanted to go down the slide, but the sign at the entrance showed a specific height requirement. Unfortunately, Parker was just a little below the mark. He was so disappointed, and it broke my heart to see him so bummed out. I told him I would go with him to the top of the slide and talk to the attendant. I thought that maybe with my sales skills and my charm, I could get him in. I explained to Parker that this might not work, but it could not hurt to ask. So up we went to the top with much anticipation. Once there, the attendant measured my son and said, sorry, but he cannot ride the slide. I gave the attendant my best sales pitch, assuring him that I would be with my son the whole time, and take full responsibility. Unfortunately, I could not change the attendant's mind. The rules are there for safety and liability reasons, and the attendant could not make an exception. Unsuccessful, we walked back down the steps together and went about the rest of the day.

The following day, we were eating lunch, and unexpectedly, Parker said to me, "Dad, I just wanted to tell you, thanks for trying to get me on the slide yesterday. You didn't have to do that, but it meant a lot." It caught me by surprise because he had not said much about the situation since it happened. I guess it just took a day to sink in and for him to reflect on it. How profound that at the age of five years old, Parker took his focus off the disappointment of not being allowed on the slide and instead chose to focus on the gratitude he felt toward me for trying to help him have that experience. His thoughtful remark is a clear reflection of the culture we have created as a family:

- Be positive
- Openly communicate our thoughts and feelings
- Express gratitude for the love we share

Now that Parker is 6, and several inches taller, you bet your ass we are going back to that slide for Parker to ride that bad-boy or find an even bigger, better adventure!

I approach my business family in much the same way. From the time I hire a person, they become part of my family. The entire team and I want everyone to feel the same type of connection for each other. Whether you are going to build a business from the ground up or buy one that is already running, you will want to establish the culture and systems that will attract and sustain top-quality team members who share your philosophy and work ethic.

> *"If you take care of your people, your people will take care of your customers, and your business will take care of itself."*
>
> ~ J W Marriott

Hiring the right people and developing them to their highest level is key to any business's success. Determine their natural strengths and passions then match them up with the appropriate position within your organization. Challenge your team members to grow. Provide the tools and environment that fosters advancement. Praise them publicly and often. If you must address a personnel issue, give them the respect and dignity to do it privately. I also believe that it's vital to enjoy your job, so I try to keep our culture light and fun while growing and serving our customers. Conduct meetings with a purpose. Use that time to energize and excite them about the company mission and equip each one to overcome any objections or obstacles. Simon Sinek tells us that both customers and employees will be loyal and believe in you if they first understand *why* you do what you do before they know the *how* or *what* of your business. Immerse your work family in a culture rich with communication, respect, acknowledgment, and validation. They will either flourish or opt-out.

If you are a business owner, you have experienced that right-hand man or woman who was "everything" to your business, your customers loved them, or they were the face of the company. You were sure they would take you to the next level, but instead, either you had to let them go, or they decided to leave your organization. If this has not happened to you yet, it will. The first time it occurred in my business, I cried myself to sleep, thinking, "The world is over! How am I going to do this without them?" But by the tenth time it happened, I was confident that everything would be okay. The difference was experience and systems. Through those earlier instances, which felt like devastating losses, I learned to hire slow, fire fast, and develop succession plans to ensure my company's continuity regardless of the individual in any one position.

> *"Everybody is a genius. But if you judge a fish by its ability to climb a tree, it will live its whole life believing that it is stupid."*
> ~ Albert Einstein

Being able to recognize a person's strengths and match them up with the position that best suits those talents paves the way for maximum growth. One of my favorite examples of this is my Chief Financial Officer (CFO), Erin Gust. She is fantastic! Erin is my right hand in everything that I do. When I met her, she was taking care of kids in the daycare I own, but I could tell it just wasn't her thing. One day I asked her how we could expand the daycare. I thought that she might have a few ideas about things we could improve since she worked there.

A day or two later, she came back to me with a whole book of ideas! It looked to me like she had done several weeks' worth of work on this, but to her, it was a chance to shine. Her report clearly showed me how much she loved facts and figures. It all came so naturally to her, and at that time, numbers were like a foreign language to me. I could never have analyzed all that data and come up with such a thorough business expansion plan in such a short amount of time.

I immediately offered her a job in operations. She quickly worked her way up and proved herself indispensable. The growth I witnessed in her made me realize that my organization needed a CFO. She was unquestionably the right choice for the position. She now runs the financial side of ALL of my businesses. I sincerely admire her because her brain works the opposite of mine. She's a financial person who loves to think in numbers all day long, and she loves paper. She is incredible at analyzing and translating the data into meaningful guidance for my companies' direction, and everything she does protects the culture and future of the company.

Discovering Erin's strength and passion allowed her and me to realize her true potential. Crafting various operations and financial positions that Erin grew through, established a career path for her and built the infrastructure I needed for my companies. Jobs cost money to create and sustain, but if implemented correctly, they pay for themselves through cost containment. Putting her in the correct position has allowed her to advance beyond what we both imagined. She no longer lumbers through a job that did not suit her, and I have more financial stability than ever.

We all have our strengths and weaknesses, and my talents are in sales and inspiration. While I love to challenge myself, my shortcomings are absolutely paperwork, follow-through, and follow up. I am always working to bring in the next dollar; however, I realize that without the proper infrastructure, it could all fall out from underneath. I learned a long time ago to protect my blind spots by hiring people smarter than me. As a business owner, I challenge you to review your organization and find the hidden gems already working for you who need to be put into their best fit positions so they can achieve their greatness.

To further demonstrate this point, here's a quick story about Isaiah Gonzales. He's an integral part of our organization. Isaiah started with me as a 20-year-old personal trainer, working with clients. He then moved into selling personal training and grew into a front desk spot, later becoming a General Manager of Snap Fitness. Now, Isaiah is the General Manager of Snooze Mattress Company. He's one of the most motivated and hardest working people I know and has earned every promotion. In just four years, he's worn many completely different hats, filling various roles while searching for his perfect position. He's still not done growing, but for now, it's an ideal assignment for him. There's a strong possibility that Isaiah's next job hasn't even been created yet.

I can tell story after story of how people have moved from business to business or position to position within my companies. Still, I can't reiterate enough how critical it is to get the fish out of the trees and help find its water!

Outside experts have also saved me a lot of time. Instead of spending the time to learn something that is entirely beyond my scope, I find someone who specializes in that area and delegate the job to him or her. For instance, I am currently working on a project that requires legal and tax advice. While I have been researching and learning about the concept at a high level, it is not prudent to master all the intricate details. I need to know enough to direct the professionals to transform my idea into reality and comprehend the options they present so I can make an informed decision about the final product. In other words, let the experts be experts and don't be a control freak.

Set clear goals and expectations for your teams. I often discuss our results with my team then challenge them to assess our progress and identify areas they think we can improve. We will set a new goal, and they will create a 30-day action plan to achieve it. The problem-solving sessions could sound like "if our goal is to make 100 sales:

- we either close 70% of the people that come in; then we need to work backward to know that we need 143 of people to walk into the doors,
or
- if we can increase our closing percentage to 80%, we only need 125 potential new customers coming in to hit our goal".

Either way, we can still achieve that 100 new member goal. We also will discuss contingency plans so that if, for some reason, we're short, we have a system to make sure that we call and follow up with every potential customer that has been in and not bought previously. We don't just throw a pie in the sky number out there without talking through how we can realistically reach that level. We brainstorm creative and new ideas to generate additional leads or sales.

Don't be afraid to learn from the new guy. Sometimes, the greenest associate brings a fresh perspective and sees things through a different lens. They may also have a different experience from their previous employer. It doesn't matter whether it's day one or day one hundred of them working for me, I always welcome new ideas. If someone can show me a better way to accomplish something and sell me on the idea, I'm open to it. I will change everything we have done in the past if the new way is more efficient or effective.

In terms of creating and implementing systems, if that is not your forte, I recommend hiring an expert to assist you because the long term benefits will far outweigh the initial investment cost. Even trainers or athletes who are the best in the world, like Michael Jordon, have coaches. One of the smartest things that I ever did was find my coach Dave Garcia who excels at developing systems. Every week we review any areas of the businesses that need attention. For instance, one time, I had an employee steal from the company. My systems coach and I analyzed how it happened, and we created a system to close the loophole he had found in our structure. Now, I don't have to worry about that issue again. We have addressed issues around screening in our hiring process. We have developed extensive training programs that ensure the seamless flow of resources through the company, which improves quality and minimizes the impact of turnover. We have constructed policies that support and grow the culture of my business environment. There hasn't been a problem or challenge we have encountered that we couldn't design a system to handle.

I take a lot of pride in our hiring process. Over the years, I have interviewed thousands of people. One of the most important factors to me is, "does this individual match our culture and integrity, will they fit into our family. Are they fun and a little bit weird?" As part of the mentoring program and succession plan, I often invite staff members to observe the interview process when filling a vacant position. I teach them how to ask questions, listen for the answers, and the value of non-verbal communication. I learned a tremendous amount about interviewing in my job when I was allowed to observe and debrief with my manager afterward. I found it an invaluable training tool. After watching an interview, my team members and I discuss the questions I asked, the meaning behind them, and the information I gain from the answers. Including my team demystifies the selection process and enhances their interpersonal skills.

Part of building your team includes the people outside of the business organizations you can rely on for advice, support, and expertise to augment your own. You have probably heard the theory that the five or so individuals in your inner circle have the most significant influence on you. There is even a belief that your income is the average of the five people closest to you. I tend to expand that notion and think more about the metaphor of a bus. You are the driver of your bus, and the seats are limited. You need to pay attention to whom you give a place on your bus. They will inspire and influence you and your family. It is imperative to help each other grow and have fun along the journey. Be sure to include your mentors, coaches, pioneers, and role models.

WHO'S ON YOUR BUS? EXERCISE

Take a few minutes right now and think about who is <u>already</u> on your bus.

- Who are your biggest influencers?
- Who are your loudest critics?
- Whose voice do you hear in your head when you are working through a tough decision?
- Who encourages you?
- Who tries to stop you?
- Where do you turn for strength or inspiration?
- Do you have role models?
- Who is your accountability partner?
- Who do you trust most with your hopes and fears?
- Who supports your dreams?
- Who are your cheerleaders?
- Who puts you down?
- Who uplifts you?
- Who challenges you?
- Who makes you feel better about yourself, just by spending time with them?

All of these folks are impacting you daily, whether you realize it or not. They are the opinions you hear and the approving and disapproving looks you get from family and friends in your everyday encounters or from your childhood memories. They are present in the choices you make, and they feed the self-talk that plays in your head subconsciously.

Now ask yourself, are all of these the people the ones you want on your bus going forward. You get to choose! Just like getting rid of a bad employee. If you don't, it will kill your culture. This may sound harsh, but if you need to kick someone off your bus to stay positive and on your path, then do it!

Focus your energy on developing the relationships that feed your soul and support your goals, only allowing those that have your best interest at heart to impact you. Nurture those people in your life. It's the supportive and positive people in your life that cheer you on with uplifting messages. When you focus only on the beneficial messages, you stay on course to achieve your highest aspirations.

Just like the other lessons in this book, this lesson is full of incredible information. Were you shocked to discover that ultimately you're responsible for everything at home and in business? The great news is that you don't have to do it all alone. Envision the qualities of your ideal work environment and healthiest family dynamics. The people are the 'who and the why.' Culture and Systems are the 'how.' The quality of the culture you create, the integrity of the people in your life, and the cutting-edge systems you implement are your domain. That's one of the coolest and most exciting parts of building your dream. These components are also the tools you need to turn your vision into your best life. Having so much responsibility can be mind-boggling. Does it sound overwhelming? It could be if you didn't have the tools and strategies from this lesson. Jump on the attack maneuvers below and get started today. Set your sights on areas that will result in the most significant impacts first.

Who's On Your Bus?

Key Lesson Takeaways

- ✓ Envision your ideal work environment and go build it!
- ✓ Imagine your healthiest family dynamics and create it!
- ✓ Share your Why with your family and teams
- ✓ Have fun
- ✓ Do the "Who's on Your Bus?" Exercise
- ✓ Hire slow, fire fast
- ✓ Communicate

Jenny's Advice

In marriage and business, you are most powerful when you rely on the strength of those around you. The Bus exercise was the best thing I ever did, but it was also the hardest. Make sure your bus is full of people who make you a better human.

LESSON 8
Growth

Photo by Jeremy Bishop

Growth

Gaur Gopal Das, a former Hewlett Packard engineer, now a captivating Indian lifestyle coach and motivational speaker, tells a parable of 'The King and Two Falcons'. There was a King who received a pair of majestic Peregrine falcons. He hired an expert trainer to work with the two amazing birds. After some time, one of the falcons was soaring gracefully over the castle while the other sat motionless. He appeared glued to the branch. Was he unable or merely unwilling to fly? Was he afraid to explore? He had not moved since the trainer had begun working with the pair. His Highness tried everything, bringing resources from all over the kingdom, but no one could get the bird to fly. He decided the quandary called for someone who understood the ways of nature and birds to help his falcon. He sent a representative out into the countryside to find and enlist such a person. The very next morning, the king woke to see both gorgeous falcons flying above the gardens. He immediately sent for the aide and demanded an audience with the miracle worker who had taught the second bird to fly.

Standing before the surprised and grateful Ruler was a humble farmer. His Majesty inquired, "How did you teach my falcon to fly when he would not leave that branch?" The farmer replied simply, "I cut down the branch."

The lesson here is that we are all meant to fly! We all have astounding potential, beyond our imagination and far beyond our everyday existence. Unfortunately, so many of us are stuck clinging to the comfort of familiar environments. What is the branch holding you back from flying? Identify and chop down whatever is preventing you from your full potential. Don't let your fears or weaknesses stop you from taking risks necessary for your growth!

Real growth begins at the edge of your comfort zone, so don't limit yourself to only the safe and tested path, try things that scare and challenge you. Are your dreams being held back by fear? What adventures do you wish you could experience? Ask yourself, why haven't you done them? Is there a small step you can take in the direction of your dream or aspiration? Maybe that means signing up for that computer class at the community college that you have wanted to take but are nervous about trying. Perhaps you have always wanted to run a marathon, climb a mountain, or captain a boat. Whatever you want to do, if you are passionate about it, you can find a way to realize your vision.

Start small and gain momentum or jump into the deep end and completely go for it! If not now, then when? There are numerous resources available to help you get started and assist you along your journey. Mentors and coaches are priceless when it comes to helping you fly. They won't accept excuses. They'll guide you to get clear on your 'why' and hold you accountable.

I was afraid to be in politics, but I had a passion for giving back to my community in that way. So I pushed myself beyond my comfort zone and ran for an elected official position on the Pueblo West Metro Board. Fourteen candidates, many of whom were politicians, were running for three open seats. Not only did I win, I took first place!! It's not only about winning or losing; it's about overcoming your fears. I could've just as easily lost that race as been victorious. It was my willingness to put myself out there and try that made all the difference. Never trying is an automatic loss and reinforces your fears. Now that I have faced that fear, I can serve my community in a way that I could never have before. I am a valued board member because I bring a different perspective and collective experience to the room. My hometown of Pueblo means the world to me. I dedicate my energy to ensure it grows and prospers.

You never know what you can achieve unless you try. These two quotes from Thomas Edison help illuminate the moral of this lesson: "*I have not failed. I've just found 10,000 ways that won't work.*" and "*Many of life's failures are people who did not realize how close they were to success when they gave up."* A person with grit believes that failure is a temporary state and that they can learn to do it differently. Whenever you attempt something that you fear or shy away from, you are silencing that negative inner voice that limits your willingness to take chances.

Several of my lessons come into play when it comes to growth. You must have a clear and strong enough why, you must be of a positive mindset, and you need to have determination or grit. Why is your first step, belief, or having your head in the right frame of mind is the second step in overcoming fears and achieving your dreams. The third step is determination, which keeps you trying new things.

WHY + POSITIVITY + DETERMINATION = GROWTH

After an epic sailing trip in the British Virgin Islands with one of my best friends, Chris, and our families, we discovered we were hooked on sailing. Unfortunately, it can be expensive to hire the boat, captain and crew. We knew we were definitely going to do this trip again, but next time we wanted to be in control. After doing some research, we realized how much we could save and how much fun it would be if we could Captain the boat ourselves. We both have grit, so we dove in headfirst. We spent ten days immersed in classes that required book study and actual sailing practice. Chris is a lawyer; he's smart, can remember tons of information, and doesn't break a sweat about tests. He was more concerned with the required hands-on portion of the certification process. If you don't know me by now reading, retaining information and test-taking are all challenges, so I had to study extra hard and read the material several times. I've always been good at learning by doing, so no pun intended, I sailed through the hands-on part. Throughout the course, we stayed positive and determined to get our licenses. By the end, Chris and I each earned 3 Captain's licenses, and now we can rent boats anywhere in the world.

We both overcame any fears or apprehension we had because our Why, wanting to have sailing vacations with our families was so strong. We both believed we could do it, and we remained positive throughout the challenge. And finally, determination brought us over the finish line: these three pieces are the formula for growth.

Apply this formula to your own life. I've used this to help me buy homes and businesses, retire early, run a marathon, jump out of a plane, and even have a dance-off with my wife in front of thousands of people. Whatever you want to accomplish, don't let anything stop you from growing. Push your limits!

There are many ways to push your limits and grow. In business and life, challenging your philosophy or *the way you've always done something* can result in unexpected benefits. Paying yourself first is hard for most business owners because we can't wrap our minds around choosing to pay us first and others afterward. Our nature is to care for others first, and as a person, that's a great trait, but in business, it can limit us.

> Many people talk about the concept of *pay yourself first.*

One of the best books I have ever read on the subject was "Profit First" by Mike Michalowski. Still, it took my coach Dave, almost a year of hammering me with the idea before I stopped long enough to digest the information and get on board. Now that I've finally implemented this for myself, I fully comprehend the importance of this principle. It completely changed my mindset and decision-making process. Instead of feeling self-sacrificing, I felt empowered to make more forward-thinking choices and to lead the company in a more progressive direction. If you're a business owner and you don't pay yourself a salary yet, find a way to make this change today. When you leave yourself until last and take from the leftovers, you continually reinforce to your subconscious mind that you're not worthy. That feeling will trigger a cycle that can sabotage your personal progress and business growth.

Does public speaking hold you back from your dreams? It's one of the most common barriers to success. Are you one of the 10% of people who love to talk in front of groups? Or, are you in the 73% who have anxiety or outright fear when it comes to speaking in public? Some people are more afraid of public speaking than they are of dying. The National Institute of Mental Health indicates that people fear being judged, and the distress exhibits in the form of mild nervousness, sweaty hands, or more severe physical responses. As a Toastmaster member, I've learned tools and techniques to speak with anyone about any topic. I took this step to reduce the amount of nervousness I previously experienced, and my confidence in public speaking has dramatically increased. I attributed my nervousness to a natural human reaction. Honestly, I still don't love public speaking, but I am getting better.

I acknowledge that there are always components of a business or industry that I need to learn to succeed. For instance, I have never really been a numbers guy. I don't know if I thought numbers were beyond my abilities or if it was an apprehension from childhood that I continued to feed over the years. I knew I had to charge ahead and overcome this fear if I wanted to win in business. So, I committed myself to learn about financials. As I stuck with it and learned more about finances, my fears began to fade, and my confidence grew stronger. I now look forward to looking at the numbers for each of my businesses daily. I understand projections and have enough working knowledge of financial reports to implement any changes to adapt and avoid potential problems. Imagine how my companies would have suffered, had I not become comfortable and fluent in the language and significance of numbers. You might be a financial wizard or not. You might find another aspect of owning a business that stumps you or that you avoid.

My advice, do not procrastinate another minute. There are many ways to learn what you need to know.

- Ask an expert
- Attend a seminar
- Tap into local resources
- Ask questions
- Read or listen to a book on the topic
- Listen to relevant podcasts
- Watch Youtube videos
- Google can teach you anything

You do not have to be an expert, but you do need to have a basic understanding to know what your expert is recommending or telling you, otherwise you won't be able to execute the appropriate changes.

There are many more ways to acquire knowledge in this age of information and technology than ever before. Do you know how you learn best? Are you stronger in visual, auditory, or kinesthetic skills? I know I'm an auditory learner, which means that I absorb information significantly more quickly and clearly when I hear rather than read it. That's why I prefer to listen to books on Audible or listen to a Podcast or even watch an informational YouTube video. Many people say, "Google it" when they want to look something up. I say, "YouTube it!" Back when I struggled and failed with college courses, I thought I just couldn't learn at the pace needed to keep up. Since discovering my auditory learning strength, I am amazed at how much more material I can digest. I highly recommend you identify and leverage your learning styles.

- <u>Visual learners</u> find it easier to comprehend and remember things through pictures, graphs, charts, reading, or other visual material. Ask yourself, "Do I solve problems by writing or drawing diagrams?"
- <u>Auditory learners</u> find it easier to comprehend information when they listen to it. They often gravitate toward the spoken word, sounds, music, rhythm, and rhymes. Ask yourself, "When I need to remember a list of items, do I remember it by repeating it over and over out loud?"
- <u>Kinesthetic of Experiential learners</u> benefit from physical sensations, movements, and interactions, including hands-on opportunities, such as writing, drawing diagrams, and using role-play. Ask yourself, "Do I learn how to do something best by trying to do it myself?"

Once you identify your learning strength, you can easily set yourself up for success. Next, you can help your family and business teams become aware of their styles.

The approach I take for myself is the same one that I utilize to address professional development for each of my business managers and their respective teams. I challenge each individual to identify their weak side and conquer it. I provide support, feedback, and accountability throughout the growth process, ensuring that all issues, not just the easy ones, get addressed, and nothing gets swept under the rug. I mentor everyone the way my coaches mentor me.

I pitch different scenarios to the team every day to help them grow and improve. I might say, "This is what we achieved last week. Now, I want everyone to come up with creative ways to help us surpass last week's results." We challenge ourselves by setting the bar even higher. Together the team figures out how we get there by developing an action plan and identifying the steps necessary to achieve the new goal. One of the things we will be focusing on is an actual scenario. If we lost 10% of the business during the shutdown, the challenge is how do we bring in enough for the rest of the year to recoup the loss. Is 20% enough, and how do we increase our business to generate it? These questions are critical for every business owner to ask themselves. Don't fall into the negativity trap of ,"poor me." Instead, focus on how you can thrive during these times.

Another training method I use quite often, especially with my sales teams, is role-playing. It's an impactful tool that excites, energizes, and equips my team for success. The technique helps you apply your product and company knowledge to overcome customer objections. Engaging in spontaneous role-play teaches you to think on your feet and adapt to both familiar and unique customer situations. It's simple to implement. Pair up your team members, assigning one as the sales consultant or customer service agent, and the other plays the customer. Then you provide scenarios for them to enact. It can be helpful to start with typical customer requests with a few common objections and maybe a non-verbal cue for the team member to incorporate. Each pair plays out the scene. As they hone their skills, you can increase the difficulty level of the scenario. The rest of the group can observe and, in the end, provide feedback and suggestions. What you expect to see and hear is the team member developing rapport with the customer, understanding their concern or request, probing further into the situation, then offering a solution or alternative that satisfies the customer.

In role-playing with a group, there is always someone who excels at each product, upgrade, or customer objection. It makes sense that they become the teachers or leaders for that round. Rarely is one person the expert in all aspects of any one job, so team members take turns demonstrating role-plays where they have been extraordinarily successful. This practice helps the team members grow by learning from each other's strengths.

Keep in mind that role-playing can be uncomfortable for your team initially, but if they practice, it will improve their skills and increase their confidence. A prime example is our current Snap Fitness Assistant Manager, Nicole. When we started role-playing as part of the daily team training, she was so nervous she would physically shake. Now, one year and lots of practice later, Nicole leads most of the role plays WITH CONFIDENCE. Just repeat, repeat, and repeat again!

COVID-19 and the global pandemic requiring total lock-downs provided a unique opportunity to focus on professional and personal development for me, my family, and business teams. I committed to keeping my staff on the payroll through the shutdown, I also committed to making the time productive. As part of professional growth and development, we discussed my vision for the future of our companies, I listened to their feedback, and incorporated their ideas. Maintaining connections was vital during this time, so we scheduled daily Zoom Video calls for each group. Those calls included:

- Book Club Discussion
- Trouble-shooting
- Creative Solutions
- Question of the Day
- Big Picture Items
- Lots of fun

For each of my teams, I started a book club. Each week we read a different personal development or business book such as:

- Rich Dad, Poor Dad by Robert Kiyosaki
- Who Moved My Cheese by Dr. Spencer Johnson
- How to Win Friends and Influence Others by Dale Carnegie
- Delivering Happiness by Zappos Founder, Tony Hsieh
- The Book of Joy by Dalai Lama and Desmond Tutu, with Douglas Abrams
- TED Talks (GRIT, WHY)
- Read the article on 1%

When we met to discuss the material, those conversations went far beyond typical Question and Answer sessions. They became deep dives into the topics and how we could weave these new concepts in our existing culture. On the same calls, we tackled a problem or challenge of the day. This part of the call generated innovations around business practices, marketing, customer service, and even new product ideas. We're currently exploring a patent and prototype for a new product in the sleep industry. To round out the calls, we shared our answers to the "Question of the day," which could be:

- Try meditation tonight, and tomorrow tell us about your experience.
- Which superpower would you choose and why?
- Most influential person in your life and why?
- If you could be a famous person for a day, who would it be and why?

Everyone loved the opportunity it provided to grow. According to the feedback, there were even more significant benefits realized. Team members were able to observe and get to know each other in ways that we would never have made time to do during a typical workday. What started as a way to keep my teams engaged during this unprecedented time turned into tremendous growth, great love, and respect for each other, and we morphed from workgroups into a family. We became closer during the shutdown than we could have without it. That was the design, but I never realized how deep it would go until it unfolded. The changes that took place for each of us on a personal level and as a team during this time will impact the rest of our lives. My businesses may have lost a lot of money during the mandatory quarantine, but what we gained in growth and connections will put us so much farther ahead when reopening as the world finds its new normal. We will be able to work together and serve our customers at such an elevated level because of how we spent the time apart.

During COVID-19, did you just watch a ton of Netflix and Facebook or challenge yourself to grow you, your family, and business? What did you learn from this time, and how can you use it to create a more robust, more productive experience for you and those in your life? I know that working from home so consistently has opened my eyes to the benefits of remote work. I don't see myself returning to my old work style after this is over. Before, I thought I was balancing my life well; now, I'm upgrading my whole approach to where and how I spend my time.

Another benefit of spending lock-down time at home is what I've noticed about my kids. You can learn so much from your children if you just watch and listen. One of the coolest things about being a dad is watching your children grow. Children's love for knowledge and the ability to take risks is second to none. From a young age, they always want to try different things, from climbing something new to putting anything in their mouth. Why? Well, because they are curious and eager to discover and experience the world. A child's parents and their environment have a significant influence on them. If we, as parents, are always trying new things and giving our children a chance to use their imagination daily, they will grow up to dream. Hopefully, if we do our job right ... they will DREAM BIG and not worry what others think. The more children use their brains to solve their problems and think up new creations to draw, build, or act out, the more they will do the same as adults.

Adults often struggle to recapture the pure innocence of a child's mind. The beginner's mind is a kind of clean slate, with an openness to new ideas, eagerness to learn, a comfort in not knowing everything or even anything. It only exists before we allow the flood of concocted preconceived notions or fabricated fears from past experiences to interfere with the pure joy of learning and exploration.

Do you remember the freedom you felt as a child? Wasn't there a time when you would dance, run, laugh, play, sing, and not care where you were or what anyone thought? Think about the time when you just knew you could be and accomplish anything. If someone told you no, you couldn't even wrap your mind around it. No wasn't in your vocabulary, because everything was possible.

Every day, my four-year-old daughter Paisley dances with such a carefree spirit and not a worry in the world. She'll dance anywhere, on top of a table, or even in the grocery store. I can't help but smile as I see my precious little girl, dressed in her princess costume, dancing uninhibited and from the heart. I never want her to lose her free spirit. I know she might feel pressure to take on societal norms of conforming to expectations. Can we prevent our children from losing that judgment-free expression? As a dad, I'm going to do everything in my power to help her stay true to herself, because it's that free spirit that allows us to remain creative, growing, and happy.

Parker, who's all of five years old, will debate you if you tell him no. It doesn't matter what you say no about, he'll have 200 reasons why he can do it or why it will work. Parker sees himself as capable of doing everything, and it makes no sense to him that sometimes we don't see it the same way. He's brilliant at overcoming objections, and he doesn't give up. Talk about determination. It's our job as parents to keep his world of possibilities alive for-ever! I don't want him to lose that. I worry, "Will there be a No that he hears that will shut him down and make him give in?"

At only one-year-old, Preston is at the early stages of development. His conscious memories of this age will fade while his current emotions form the basis for who he is becoming and his personality. You can see the strength of his bond with his mom because he lights up every time he's in her presence. There's no agenda on his part, just an unconditional love that supersedes all else. Can we prevent him from losing that feeling? If so, How? Will that feeling grow with him, or will he outgrow it?

My why, of 'family first,' means that it's my responsibility to prevent any limitations on my children's dreams or growth. The same is true for my team members and companies. I'm their advocate; it's my job to nourish their growth and give them every advantage to surpass whatever vision they have for themselves.

Be a champion for yourself and those in your life. Don't let society, negative friends, or family dictate who you can be or how far you can go. If someone tells you 'no,' find a way to the yes. Remember, **the answer is Yes, the question is How**. Growth happens every day, so be the plant that grows a little more than the rest. Discover the right environment for you to thrive and then create the reality you deserve.

Key Lesson Takeaways

- ✓ Make a list of your dreams, goals, aspirations
- ✓ Identify what keeps you from realizing them
- ✓ Create a plan with action steps
- ✓ Find the best resources available
- ✓ Be open to learning
- ✓ Stay curious, ask why and why not
- ✓ Be obsessed with growth
- ✓ Break the branch!
- ✓ Try the One-Day Rule. It's a great way to kick-start your next level of growth. Carve out a full 8 hour day and do as much as you can on your dream. Don't allow yourself to be distracted by anything else. You'll be stunned at your progress. I could write a whole book, just about this method, stay tuned...

Jenny's Advice

Being with someone who dreams big and thrives on growth means that you're in for a lot of adventures! So, dreamers, your spouse is your partner in life, respect them, and include them in the big decisions before you make them. Supporting partners, be open-minded, and listen with an open heart. That's how you allow your big-dreamer to chase their dreams with you as their first mate.

LESSON 9
Integrity and Gratitude

> *"Integrity is fundamental to family and business. Without Integrity and your word nothing else matters"*
>
> ~ Matt Smith

What does integrity mean to you? What do you think of when you hear the word gratitude? Integrity and gratitude are states of being that each requires you to walk the walk day in and day out. These two qualities demand you to be a person of honor. They are the keystone of being a good human. Do integrity and gratitude guide your life? It's okay if it takes you time to answer this question. It challenges you to look at the overarching way in which you lead your life. Practice integrity and gratitude even when no one is watching.

I've come to understand that my word means everything in my relationships, and my actions must support my words. Regardless of my role as a parent, husband, business owner, politician, or friend, everyone knows that I am true to my word.

Integrity and Gratitude

If you teach your kids nothing else in this world, **"Teach them to be good humans!"** By good humans, I mean knowing right from wrong, doing the right thing for the right reason, admitting when they are wrong, and apologizing. Instilling a moral compass is our job as parents. While they can reinforce the messages, we can not rely solely on teachers, coaches, books, YouTube, or educational TV. As early as possible, integrity should be a part of the conversation. Likewise, you must demonstrate and practice gratitude with your children to fill and strengthen their spirit. Gratefulness can be the difference between coming through a difficult time stronger or getting stuck. Gratitude makes for happier, more positive people.

There will be opportunities along the way for you to witness how you are doing at teaching these lessons and how well your children have embraced the concepts. I recently had one of those moments. My kids wanted a slumber party in our basement, and although they are still pretty young, I agreed. I was willing to give it a try and see how it played out. As I was getting them set up with pillows and blankets, I gave them a quick dad-speech about my behavior expectations. Reminding them that this was the first time and if they broke the rules or didn't behave well,

> **They both nodded in agreement, and then there was a pause, they looked at each other and said, "Dad, we need to tell you something."**

it could be the last time they were allowed to have a slumber party.

Immediately, my internal dad's danger siren blared in my mind. I thought, "Oh no, what could they have to tell me?", the party hadn't even begun. They told me, "We brought candy downstairs, and we were probably not supposed to." Boom, it hit me, the lessons Jenny and I had been teaching them were taking root. I was so thankful; they were honest and willing to accept responsibility for their actions. Even though I might have never discovered their candy stash, at that moment, they chose to come clean. They knew that it could end the slumber party and have additional consequences. It was such a profound moment for me as a dad. My kids had unknowingly created an integrity test for themselves, and they passed it with flying colors. They're kids, so they're still learning, but I know that they won't sneak the candy the next time because it's against the rules. In a flash, they revealed to me the strength of their characters.

I asked them if they thought the candy was a good idea, and they agreed that it was not, and they felt bad for taking it. I told them how proud I was of them for being honest with me, which was much more important than the candy anyway. I let them have some of it before I tucked them in. That night was significant; it was a win/win. They demonstrated they knew right from wrong and had the courage and integrity to own up to it. This example may seem small, but these are precisely the kinds of occasions we as parents need to keep an eye out for because they deserve our attention. These moments are when we get to celebrate progress, or course correct and reinforce the lessons. Do you notice when your kids exhibit integrity and do you praise them?

Another story about my kids that happened recently, Paisley, my four-year-old daughter, used her allowance to buy herself a unicorn. Preston, my one-year-old son, immediately fell in love with the brightly colored, soft, stuffed toy, and he kept trying to take it for himself. Of course, Paisley cried when he wouldn't give it back. She knew she earned it, and it belonged to her. I explained to Preston that the unicorn was his sister's, and if he wanted to play with it, he needed to ask permission. Of course, Preston was sad, being only one year old, and I pointed out to Paisley that he wasn't old enough to earn an allowance and couldn't buy himself the unicorn.

Parker, my oldest, watched this happen for a few days. The next time he had the opportunity to spend his allowance shopping online, Parker decided to buy a unicorn for Preston so they could each have one, and be happy. I was extremely impressed that he had not only been observant enough to identify the problem but also wanted to provide a solution. I asked him, "Are you sure you want to do that? That's very nice, but you won't be able to get anything for yourself this week." His reply blew me away. At age five, my son said, "That's okay Dad, I would rather see Preston and Paisley both happy now, and I can wait until next week for my stuff." He's compassionate and wise beyond his years! Sure, I could have bought Preston a unicorn, but the fact that Parker chose to buy it for his siblings meant so much more. It was quite a proud Dad moment

In business, numerous situations will test your ethics. Character tests come in all shapes and sizes. In some cases, there will be a temptation to follow a lesser path, thinking to yourself, it's small, no one gets hurt, or no one will know. Over time these seemingly insignificant yet poor decisions accumulate, eroding your sense of self, leading to deceitful patterns. Always take the high road! I want you to avoid unnecessary remorse because it will eat away at your identity. It's far better to be a person of integrity who can feel proud of their actions and achievements rather than one who regrets how they got there. You want to earn the respect and admiration of your family and employees.

Being a person of integrity also means following through on your commitments. If you say you are going to do something, DO IT! Too many people over-promise but then fail to deliver. Over time, the disappointments undermine your credibility and breed distrust or discontent among your team. In the past, I was guilty of this because I was disorganized. Promises and commitments fall through the cracks when you're unorganized. Unfortunately, dropping the ball like this can spiral out of control very quickly. You don't want to be known as the person who forgets and doesn't see it through. Sincere intentions without deliberate actions will get you nowhere. It's almost embarrassing how chaotic I used to be, and how often I would forget things we discussed.

An employee had won a monthly challenge, and the prize was a gift card. I didn't have the gift card on hand to award on the day I announced the winner of the contest. Instead, I told them I would have the gift card soon. I had sincere intentions of picking it up, but I kept forgetting. Time passed, and the employee asked about it, and I again assured them that I would pick it up. After a while, the employee was probably uncomfortable to ask again, and I'm sure, felt frustrated because it came across as an empty promise. What employee would ever participate in a contest going forward? My lack of action and organization demonstrated to this employee that they weren't important enough for me to follow through. That was a wakeup call for me. I never want anyone in my life to feel this way.

You have to deliver on your promises and do it promptly. If you're going to offer an incentive or bonus, have it BEFORE you start the contest. My solution was to create a better system by delegating that responsibility. Now I don't ever have to worry about being late with a reward again. My CFO, who is very organized, buys all the gift cards and bonus prizes.

Running contests to reach work goals can be energizing and fun, but only if you do your part first. You want your employees to participate, but they won't enjoy it if they don't believe you or if history has shown them that a prize doesn't exist.

Another aspect of integrity is being fully in the moment and making the people in your life a priority. For example, if you ask someone. "How's your day going?" Listen to their answer. I mean, whole-heartedly listen, because you care about the information they are sharing with you. Don't start talking over them. Don't spend that time thinking about what you're going to say next or trying to top their story. If you care but don't believe you have the time to listen, you need to re-evaluate your priorities and scheduling. Make sure you budget time for people; because relationships require nurturing.

Spending time developing relationships isn't just about "showing up for the photo op" so you can post it on social media and perpetuate the lie that you are uber involved with your family. When you are with your family, pay attention to their needs, and engage with them completely. You can learn a great deal about your kids and your spouse if you take the time to ask questions, watch them grow, interact with them through their favorite activities, and discover the world together. Learn to speak their language. Connect on their level and stay tuned-in throughout their growth process. You can help them expand their horizons by encouraging them to take risks. Challenge them to reach beyond their limits and achieve their full potential. Integrity must be at the core of each of these interactions. Also, don't miss out on the experience of gratitude along the way.

As an adult, it's fun to be a kid for a while. The other night, while we were at Parker's football practice, Paisley asked me to climb a jungle gym tree at the playground next to us. At first, I thought, no, we are here to watch Parker play. Then I realized it wasn't going to take anything away from his experience, and I didn't want to squash her excitement. As parents, we have to be careful not to crush our children's dreams or kill their hopes by saying 'no' too often or too quickly. Instead, find a way to say yes to the opportunities that let you bond. So, Paisley and I climbed to the very top of that tree, and we had a blast together! Be spontaneous! I don't ever want to miss a chance to share those impromptu moments with my kids. Do you?

It's equally important in business to pay attention to the needs of your employees. Addressing issues with staff requires a specific level of integrity:

- How ---------> Respectfully
- When -------> Timely
- Where ------> Privately

You must gauge and acknowledge your role in whatever has gone wrong. Take responsibility and set clear expectations. Leaders who lack personal accountability prefer to ignore or minimize the issue rather than deal with it head-on. Frequently, that "do nothing" approach only contributes to a growing problem.

Being present starts with a decision and a mindset which becomes a habit; eventually, it's your strategy;

it's just how you operate. It requires discipline and a commitment to compartmentalize or set boundaries so you can be fully authentic in everything you do. If you get a phone call from work while you're at home, you need to assess if it is significant enough to sacrifice some of your family time to handle the work matter. Lay the groundwork by making it known at the office that when you are with your family, they should only reach out to you if it's unquestionably an urgent matter that requires your involvement. You would be surprised at how they can figure out a solution without you, if they need to. Likewise, you should respect your team members' time away from the office by affording them the same courtesy.

Smart Tasking, which I explain in detail in Chapter 3 - Bending Time, can be extremely advantageous. Whether you're at work or home, there are gaps of time that naturally occur when the activity you are present for hasn't begun yet, or the other participants are otherwise engaged. You'll be grateful for the "loose change" concept. It enables you to maintain your integrity with your family and your business by allowing you to focus entirely on one without losing continuity with the other.

As I have discussed in previous chapters, I use VOXER with my team as a quick and effective method of communicating with the whole group. There are many options out there; this happens to be the one I chose. Voxer works exceptionally well for me when I'm out of the office. I can stay in contact with my teams without completely interrupting my family time. My teams know that this is the quickest way to reach me and get a response. Because they are so fast, I usually listen and respond to Vox messages in a matter of minutes. VOXER connects the entire team in real-time, so if there is a question or problem and I'm not immediately available to solve it, they can work together to come up with an answer. It's fantastic when I catch up on a series of messages, and I see the problem-solving process play out and come to a resolution before I even weigh in. That's progress!

I believe the efforts and daily contributions of your team should be appreciated and rewarded in a tangible way. Some companies offer 401k or retirement options, but I want to provide more. I could not hit these targets alone, so if they help me get there, I assure them that they will be rewarded and benefit from all their hard work. Granting workers a stake in the company is a great way to show appreciation for their contributions to the bottom line, and it significantly improves engagement. An Employee Stock Ownership Plan is a popular way to structure employee ownership in a company. As part-owners, with a vested interest in the overall financial success, your staff will be more efficient in their job performance and exhibit increased accountability. Publix Super Markets is currently the largest employee-owned company in the United States, with over 200,000 members. According to Forbes Magazine, it is also the eighth-largest privately held company in the country.

I've sought expertise from a wide range of professionals, addressing some hurdles to move forward with my vision. As a business owner, I highly recommend that you look into the many ways in which you, too, can share the benefits of your success with your employees. This action speaks volumes to employees about your integrity, and you will both experience immense gratitude.

Gratitude:

- Improves self-esteem
- Makes room for positive relationships
- Increases mental strength
- Boosts physical health
- Promotes better sleep

I deeply believe in giving back to your community. I'm a pretty modest guy, so it's hard for me to write about my volunteerism, but I feel that I can't write this book and not talk about it. I give back because it's the right thing to do, not for the recognition. I try to honor my mother's generous and loving example by living with purpose and passion every day. Part of how I show my gratitude for all that I've achieved is by giving to my community in many ways. I volunteer through community and academic outreach programs. Working directly with the at-risk youth of my community allows me to be a positive role model and challenge them to strive for a brighter future.

Ask yourself, is my integrity quotient up to par? Do I have credibility with my family and business associates to be a leader? If you're not sure, solicit candid feedback from a trusted advisor.

I had worked in the mattress industry for 18 years. I knew almost all the mattress people in the southern Colorado area, and I had maintained great relationships with everyone. When I decided to open my mattress store, Snooze Mattress Company, I realized that I had two choices. First, keep moving forward, open the store, and start competing with all the other mattress stores. Let the people I worked with all those years be surprised and find out on their own. The second option, before our grand opening, I could do the right thing, and tell each person about my plans. It was important that they heard it directly from me, so I called my previous employers, including the President of the Company.

I was nervous, not knowing what types of reactions I would receive, but I felt a sense of responsibility and integrity to do the right thing by speaking with each person. After all, they were so good to me, and I left on excellent terms. So in my way of thinking, I owed a lot of people a phone call or a visit in person. For the most part, everyone was excited and understanding. Some conversations were tough, but all were 100% necessary. I'm so happy I called everyone personally, even Joe, the President of my old company said he had respect for how I handled the situation. Joe's response meant a lot to me because he's a man of integrity and he had instilled that in me for the 18 years I worked for him. As I always say, take the high road and do the right thing even if it's hard. And when the task is really hard, do it yourself. What would you have done if you were in my shoes?

Earlier I shared with you that integrity requires honor and is all-encompassing in everything you do. If you have integrity areas that could use a boost, start now, and set yourself a higher standard. Every day I strive to live up to the standards set by my mom. Introducing my kids to the concepts of giving back, integrity, and gratitude at an early age ensures that our family tradition will continue, from my mother to me, and now to my kids.

Staying positive and applying some of the maneuvers in this book helped me during the most unusual period in recent history. With many businesses struggling or going under, I pivoted my business approach, and anticipating changes in the market, even opening a marketing business. I am so grateful that I was able to stay positive for my family and my business teams from the beginning of the COVID pandemic, and that we could capitalize on the time we all had together, while apart and away from regular daily routines. We:

- Created deeper connections
- Enriched relationships
- Implemented additional healthy habits
- Introduced new cultural norms
- Expanded our tools for personal and professional growth
- Brainstormed innovative customer service and marketing concepts

- Invented new products in the sleep industry
- Exercised daily
- Explored
- Fine-tuned personal responsibility

Gratitude and the right mindset will make the difference for you, your family, and teams. You don't have to be in a global emergency to achieve incredible outcomes in your life. Wouldn't you rather be living every day in a state of gratitude and integrity? Don't delay; it's too important, so do what it takes to get you there and be sure to have fun along the way.

Key Lesson Takeaways

- ✓ Assess your Integrity Quotient
- ✓ Commit yourself to be fully present for both your family and employees
- ✓ Do what you say and follow-through
- ✓ Spend time with family and employees, having fun, and working smart
- ✓ Initiate a daily gratitude practice

Jenny's Advice

Matt inspires everyone around him to strive to be better humans. He makes me a better person. I'm grateful that his mom raised him to be the most incredible person, and I'm lucky that he's the man of my dreams. Value and appreciate your spouse, tell them one thing that you are grateful for about them every day. I admire that Matt always does the right thing. Remember to take the high road and be a role model.

LESSON 10
Memories

Photo by Ian Dooley

"You can always make more money, but you cannot make more memories."

Memories are what make us feel alive and connect us to our why. They help us relive our favorite moments with family, friends, and team members. Memories give us a peek into the future, to the person that we are destined to become. Without memories, we become stuck and we would lose sight of our purpose and our why. So why wouldn't you make the most amazing memories possible?

Why are memories so significant to me? Maybe it's because my mom passed away when I was young. Perhaps it's because I have a crazy burning passion for taking advantage of every moment I can, and time scares the shit out of me. I do know that I'm grateful for my current life, and I recognize how blessed I am to have the life I do. Every day, I pinch myself as a reminder that it's all real. Fortunately, I soak it all up, and I try to capture every incredible moment. If you haven't noticed, I choose to honor my mom's memory and my family by living a life that would make them proud.

Memories elicit emotions and trigger mental images. They're about more than remembering the past. Each memory builds upon the last, accumulating into the very foundation of who we become. The memories you create today and in the future are up to you. I want your family, employees, and friends to have strong positive memories of their experiences with you because memories are how your legacy survives. Remember your big WHY that we talked about at the beginning of this book? If your family is your big WHY, like mine, then the quality time you spend with them making amazing memories is the goal and the payoff for everything else you do.

The legacy you create for your family and employees is intended to live on beyond this lifetime. If you have children, then you know how their arrival adds a whole new dimension and perspective to life. My incredible wife Jenny and my astonishing children Parker, Paisley, and Preston fill me with such joy and gratitude that I feel a sense of duty to give them the most beautiful memories possible. I want their precious memories of our time together, and who I am as a person, to be so well-established and positive that whenever that time comes and I'm no longer here, I will continue to live on in each of them. More importantly, I want my memory to spur them on, support them, and provide confidence and comfort, just as my mom's memories do for me.

As a dad, I often have experiences that generally only happen when you have kids. If I didn't have young children, I might never have watched the movie Coco which would have been a shame. I would have missed out on an epic lesson! The Disney-Pixar film, Coco, has had a profound and lasting impact on my view of shared memories and life's purpose. Disney movies always seem to have life lessons for children and more subtle yet philosophical messages for adults. This movie is no exception. It paints an inspiring picture of the value of memories. During his adventure to the Land of the Dead, the main character, Miguel, learns the fate of deceased ancestors relies heavily on the memories kept alive by their remaining relatives in the Land of the Living. As long as someone who is still alive remembers them, their spirit lives on in the Land of the Dead. Once the living forgets them, they cease to exist altogether.

I remember settling in to watch this movie with my kids. I thought, oh sweet; this will be a fun, cute movie. Surprisingly, as we watched, I realized, this is so much more than a cartoon. It made me stop and think, "who will remember me or what I did after I am gone?" Have you ever had that thought? Take a minute right now and think about your ancestors. How much do you know about your grandparents or their parents? Every generation that came before you is somehow a part of who you are today. I was blown away by this concept of how we live on through the history and memories we create with others. It reminded me of the importance of creating positive memories with my loved ones.

Exercise:

- Watch the movie Coco, whether you have kids or not, you won't regret it!
- Pay attention to the lessons in the story.
- Ask yourself, are you spending quality time with your loved ones to create a bank of vibrant memories?
- Talk with and listen to your kids about what they learned from the movie.
- Start making more meaningful memories with the people in your life.
- Have fun and be creative.

Traditions are another way in which we create memories and keep loved ones alive. Be sure to pass them down through generations, or develop new customs to enjoy as a family and carry forward. Since the beginning of time, storytelling and verbal histories have helped keep memories and cultures alive. You can use them today, as a way to connect and communicate with your family, friends, and coworkers. Shared experiences create familial and personal histories. So, be sure to make them fun for everyone and discover unique ways to document your special moments.

When I think back over my childhood, my core family was my mom, brother Jeremy and me. Since we were kids, I have always looked up to my big brother, Jeremy; truthfully, he's still my hero. When he told me about his concept to contribute to his local community, it was no surprise to me because our mom's generous and charitable nature had a significant influence on both of us. My brother is the epitome of determination. After graduating from high school in our small town, he set out for the big city with only what he could fit in his car. Jeremy has made a pretty fantastic life in Los Angeles.

While out of town on vacation, Jeremy happened to see a Miracle League baseball field and was inspired. He felt first-hand the tremendous impact this league was making in the community. The Miracle League eliminates the traditional barriers to baseball for children with disabilities by constructing their fields out of a custom-designed rubberized turf that meets these athletes' needs while reducing injuries. In addition to playing their favorite game, the team members make new friends, find acceptance from the community, and boost their self-esteem through participating in the sport.

Discovering all of this, Jeremy embraced Miracle League's mission to provide disabled children (and adults) with the opportunity to play America's favorite pastime. Beyond the games, the goal is to engage the whole community's support and participation by pairing able-bodied "buddies" with players with disabilities.

Jeremy decided that he would find a way for his community to have a Miracle League location. Remember that determination I said ran deep in Jeremy? It took three years and more than 50 meetings to make his dream a reality, but he never gave up. To cement its success, Jeremy managed to get the LA Dodgers, the Major League baseball team, to sponsor and fund the Miracle League in Los Angeles. The Dodgers even carved out space to incorporate this specialized field within their property.

I'm proud of my brother and his commitment and dedication to bring his vision to life. This league will have far-reaching, positive effects on the local children and their families for many generations. Now that's quite a legacy!

I find that my most cherished memories help to strengthen and keep alive all the incredible emotions I felt from those experiences. To this day, I love how Jenny and I first met and developed a friendship and how our story began. The depths of these feelings and memories are a big part of the foundation of my why. I hope you have a similar experience, one that helps you to build a strong basis for your why. It's memories like my story below, of meeting Jenny that help us get through those challenging days when we need the extra motivation to keep striving for our goals.

From the moment I saw her, I knew my future-wife, Jenny, was the most beautiful woman I would ever see. We met for the first time at an "Ugly Christmas Sweater Party" then again at my Big 30'th Birthday Bash. The Colorado State Fair Crash Derby set the wheels in motion. I was having trouble finding a clunker, an old beat-up car to enter into the Derby. I posted something on social media to see if anyone had any ideas. Jenny commented that she did not have one for me, but if I found some, grab two because driving in the Derby was on her bucket list. I was instantly intrigued! I always had a bucket list, but I had never met anyone else who had one much less, talked about it. Now, I couldn't wait to spend some time with her. We agreed to do the next two "Bucket List" items together, one from her list and one from mine.

The "Blazin' Wing Challenge" was coming to our town, and we decided to enter because it was on a bucket list. You might ask, "So, what's the Wings Challenge?" The restaurant chain, Buffalo Wild Wings has something called the "Blazin' Wing Challenge." You have six minutes to eat a dozen of their famous chicken wings, **caked** in their signature "Blazin'" hot-sauce, which measures 350,000 in Scoville units or 60 times hotter than a jalapeño pepper. Complete this wild contest and you get a tee shirt and your photo on the wall of fame. That's right, no big money prize, just a tee shirt, photo and of course bragging rights.

You have to sign a waiver absolving the restaurant of responsibility **if** you begin vomiting uncontrollably or go blind. **Go blind**, yes, you read it right. I think by now you get the picture - this stuff is HOT!!

You may be shocked to discover that doing this challenge was on Jenny's bucket list, not mine. I know I'm the all-in extreme guy, but this was all her idea. You need to understand that I sweat eating those mild gas station nachos because I can't handle the heat. I was looking to impress her, so I couldn't back down from the challenge.

I knew this was going to be mind over matter because it was going to burn and hurt so bad. After the first wing, my mouth was numb. I just had to push through and five long minutes later, we were DONE! Well, at least for me, Jenny, unfortunately, ended up touching her face and could not complete the challenge. The next few hours were miserable, but nothing can prepare you for the pain the next day! Enough said.

One bucket list item, done and one to go. Next, it was my turn to pick. My choice was a Colorado 14er! What's a 14er, you ask? In mountaineering terminology in the United States, a fourteener is a mountain that meets or exceeds an elevation of 14,000 feet (4,270 m) above sea level. Colorado has the majority of fourteeners in the contiguous United States. My bucket list item is to climb 14 of these before I die! So far, I have done four, so I have ten more to go. I decided to pick this adventure because hiking a mountain would be a fantastic way to spend a big chunk of time getting to know Jenny.

We had a 3-day weekend planned to head up to my Grandma Smith's Condo in Silverthorne and attack Mt Elbert. A few days before the trip, a snowstorm dumped too much snow to complete the hike. In case we needed any help deciding if it was safe to go, my future mother-in-law, who I had not yet met, reported the weather conditions to us no less than ten times. Looking back on it now, it's quite endearing that she was so concerned about me taking her daughter up into the snowy mountains.

Not wanting to miss out on the chance to spend quality time with Jenny, I suggested we go skiing instead. As it turns out, she had only skied a few times before. Perfect!, I thought. I had a crush on this girl, and maybe I could teach her to ski. Perhaps we could even fall down the mountain together a few times, just like in the movies.

Talk about memories! That weekend turned into one of those surreal trips in which we got to know each other sincerely and deeply and had a lot of laughs. There was a beautiful moment where we held hands for the first time while crossing the street. That ski trip was where it all started for us. Now, seven incredible years later, I am even more in love with this unbelievable woman than I was that magical weekend. I am such a lucky man. The depth of our love drives my determination.

Next to marrying the love of my life, having children is by far the best thing that has ever happened to me. Initially, being a Dadpreneur came with a unique set of challenges. Imagine, trying to maintain the priority of family first with infants and toddlers, while developing multiple businesses in various states of creation, and all in diverse industries. It was quite the balancing act, especially when everything was new. I never took my awe-inspiring wife for granted. I chose to be a great partner by fully participating. I couldn't have survived that phase of life if Jenny hadn't been a great partner too. Who Jenny is, and what she continues to do for our family even today, is what makes this all work.

I am forever grateful to my Aunt Anne, my mom's sister. Like my mom, Aunt Anne is generous, loving, and gives back by making a difference around the world. She's a Nurse Practitioner who travels with the amazing Doctors without Borders and Operation Smile. When Jenny and I had our first child, my Aunt picked up her life and moved to Pueblo for the first three or four years to be close by to help. I think she felt a calling to be with us as family. Not having children of her own, the time she spent in Pueblo created special memories that will last all of us a lifetime. Her being with us gave me the next best thing to having my mom there, something my family and I will never forget! I feel so blessed.

As our family grew, I wanted to ensure I didn't miss any of the milestones, I tried to keep one basic rule in the front of my mind. Wear only one hat at a time and give 100% attention to whatever has my focus. I was grateful to be completely present in every moment, whether that was in the boardroom or at home with my family. I stuck to my schedule, which allowed me to be there for those landmark moments. I can tap into the images and feelings of each experience whenever I want, imprinting them into me forever. My children may not consciously remember all of these times, but somewhere inside, they have the knowledge, and as they grow, their memories of me take on their own life. Through the power of social media, they will have access to a sort of digital scrapbook and photo album for years to come. I am conscious of this fact as I post pictures and stories of our adventures. Oh, what I would give to see my Mom's FaceBook page if it had existed in her time!

Now that my kids are older, I value the time I spend traveling with my family. I love showing my kids the world and then seeing it through their eyes. My Mother-in-Law, who we affectionately refer to as "Grandma Goose.", a title she is quite proud of, is such an integral part of our family that she often travels with us. I want to give my kids many different experiences with their grandmother. There is something magical about the three generations discovering new adventures together. These times are part of a lifetime of memories and traditions that we are building.

Every member of my family is why I am continually challenging myself to find time hacks, hire and develop excellent team members and grow because these things allow me to spend even more time with my family creating memories. As you work on the Attack Maneuvers, keep this inspiration at the forefront of your mind. The reward you'll receive is so much greater than just the benefits to your business. Remember, every lesson in this book has both something for your family and your business.

Since I have nurtured family-like bonds with my childhood friends, my family, and now their families have many opportunities to spend time with each other. Our close-knit, extended family supports each other, has fun together, and even travels as a group. One of my best friends, Chris Turner, and his family have become our travel partners over the past three years. They are a family with high moral values who have fun and enjoy life. My wife and I feel this is who we want our kids to be around. We want this family by our side on our bus. Spending time with them, and many other positive families, in this way allows us to continue to make deposits into our memory banks. Ensure that you're engaging with everyone in your life regularly and in a meaningful way.

You might recall that I always try to find the yes to any situation. I hope you are also looking for ways to say yes. Whenever we say yes, we are opening up to positive experiences in the world. Have you ever told your family that you don't have time or money to take a trip? Saying no has a detrimental impact on you and your family. Put your family first; there is nothing more important.

Too often we make an excuse about why we can't take the trip we want to because we can't afford it. Here's a simple example of how we can reprioritize when we redefine the significance of the expense. Imagine, you have car trouble, and the mechanic says that your car needs new tires, brakes, or a transmission. Somehow, you always find the money. Shouldn't you place the same or higher priority on your family's health, growth, and development? Family vacations are an investment in your child's character and future and are instrumental in developing strong family bonds. It's not about how much you spend on the trip; it's about the quality of the time together with your family. Be creative; there are many ways to build amazing experiences that don't break the bank. Some of my fondest childhood memories were when my mom took us to the mountains. It was a simple, inexpensive trip, but produced so many happy childhood memories.

Family vacations provide a chance for you to:

- Have downtime
- Connect on a deeper level
- Create fun together
- Play games
- Go for walks or bike rides
- Have quiet talks
- Spend One-on-one time
- Forge unbreakable bonds
- Make memories of a lifetime
- Allow for spontaneity
- Enhance your child's self-esteem
- Creates the space for you to give undivided attention to your kids
- Learn new skills
- Make s'mores
- Climb trees
- Collect shells or pine cones

- Share discoveries
- Most important - Use your imagination and let your kids use theirs!

Experiences are more impactful than toys to your children. Studies show that kids who travel are more likely to do better academically and financially than those who didn't explore beyond their familiar surroundings. Many families average only one vacation a year. Across the span of a child's impressionable years, that yields approximately 15 occasions for you to leave lasting impressions with your kids before they go out into the world. If that scares you, it should, so make the most of your time with your family.

Shared experiences of fun and camaraderie can also have many of the same benefits for your work teams. You can treat them to lunch or create celebrations around business milestones or humorous events. Head to a park for a day of games and a barbeque! You can even invite their families. As long as you support the fun and friendship culture in the office, your teams will embrace the momentum and build on your ideas.

Keep business meetings positive and energizing, don't use that time to point out flaws and short-comings. No one wants to be in that type of meeting. Create an atmosphere of inclusion and gratitude. If you show your employees that you genuinely appreciate them, they will be more fulfilled and motivated to excel. Interactions between people result in memories that will either enhance or detract from the legacy you leave. Positive engagements you have with your team members, develop feel-good memories.

I take my team to many conferences throughout the year. These conferences are to learn product and company knowledge, build bonds within the team, and reward all their hard work. We focus and work hard during the day, then we have some team-building fun in the evening. It's a Win/ Win. I'm a firm believer that every conference trip pays for itself within 30 days from implementing what we learn and energizing the team to committing to becoming better.

Life is too long not to enjoy yourself and too short not to make the most of every minute you have.

In other words, don't have regrets. Everyone has something that they've missed out on, a business opportunity or expansion, a chance to acknowledge someone's achievement, a child's milestone moment. For parents who see their children part-time, it's even more essential to make the moments you do have count. You must hold yourself accountable and challenge yourself to be as available as you can. This situation is where integrity comes into play, show up when you say you will, and don't make excuses. Your goal is to be a positive influence on the memories you build. It's never too late to turn things around. My dad and I found a way to make up for some lost time when I was a child. I'm so grateful that we have a growing relationship and so many positive memories as adults. Spending time together has also created an opportunity for my father to develop a relationship with his grandchildren. My dad got a "do-over," and he's taking full advantage of that as a grandpa. My kids love Papa and Nana Smith and the memories they have created. It makes my heart smile watching them together.

If you have regrets, get off your butt and do something about it now!

Have you had any business disappointments? Maybe you've been burned by an employee. I know I have, more than once, but that just caused me to create better systems, and now I have robust processes in place to minimize theft and dishonesty. Don't get stuck in regret. There are very few if any mistakes you can make that are unrecoverable. To move forward, you must be willing to learn from your mistakes, overcome any blocks that limit you, and transform your negative experiences into better memories. As they say in Jamaica, one of my favorite places, "No problems mon, just situations."

By nature, entrepreneurs are willing to take chances that others either don't take or don't see. "An Entrepreneur is someone who jumps off the cliff and builds the plane on the way down!" Be willing to take chances and forge memories with the people in your life.

I want you to think of this book as the best sandwich on the planet. It's the perfect recipe. Everyone knows it's the bread that holds it all together. A superior sandwich requires exceptional ingredients. The Power of Why chapter acts like one of the slices of bread, and this lesson on Memories, is the other one. What you decide to put in the middle is up to you. Everything in between adds the variety, flavor, and spice of life. Great memories are the purpose of this book, and like great sandwiches also require exceptional ingredients. Through my lessons, you've learned ways to communicate better, be more positive, save time, discover your why, grow, be healthy, be grateful, have integrity, and use systems to create cultures that adapt and thrive.

Make room for positive momentum in your life, and keep working on the attack maneuvers. As you master them, you'll be more efficient, freeing up time to build additional memories with your loved ones. I have given you all the tools you need. If you have not finished every chapter in this book yet, don't waste another minute! Don't make excuses! DO IT NOW!

"Life is not measured by the number of breaths we take, but by the moments that take our breath away."

None of us know how many breaths we get in a lifetime, so make the most of yours.

Memories

Start today by taking 30 minutes to reflect on the stories in this lesson. Ask yourself the questions below and write down three ways to create lasting memories at home, at work, and in relationships.:

- ✓ What memories have shaped you?
- ✓ What kinds of memories am I creating with the people in my life?
- ✓ What mark will I leave on my family, business community, and the world?
- ✓ What memories do I have of others, that I keep alive?
- ✓ What will my legacy be?

Jenny's Advice

I love capturing photos of the moments of our adventures. Life goes by so quickly. Before you know it, your kids are grown, out of the house, and creating their own lives. Maximize every moment, spending time with those you love.

Final Words

Congratulations, you did it!

Now that you've read all or parts of this book, have you started practicing, embracing, and implementing the strategies from my life lessons? Or, are you still stuck out on your branch, clinging to your comfort zone? Your dream life is waiting for you. Go get it!

As any personal trainer would say, or rather yell in your face: MOVE YOUR BUTT!! All progress occurs outside the comfort zone. If you need a little extra encouragement, imagine that I am standing in your personal space, up close, in your face. Can you feel my breath on you? All 6'4" of me is staring down at you. I'm focusing every ounce of my energy on moving you from where you are now, wishing and hoping for something better, into actions that will propel you to your best life.

I have repeatedly proven that I can make any business successful while keeping my family a priority. I've given you my tested formula for the unavoidable balancing act that comes with being a Dad-preneur because I want you to have an outstanding existence. I've explained my strategy and philosophy and shared stories to demonstrate my lessons. Each mission concludes with Key Lesson Takeaways for you to implement.

While each chapter stands on its own with a message, strategy, and actionable steps, the common thread running through this book is that everything is connected. The other common factor is you. You need to attack each activity with the same high level of intensity and keep pushing forward until you realize your vision. Apply that same level of commitment and determination to each aspect of your family and business life, and you will achieve unimaginable success across the board and be living your BEST LIFE!

From the bottom of my heart, I appreciate the time you spent with my book. I hope that you discovered valuable tips, tools, and nuggets of information to incorporate into your life. Please consider passing this book along to someone else it can help. Let's help other Dad-entrepreneurs be better in every part of their lives and guide their kids to become even better humans.

I have to take one final moment to share a story about one of my best friends, Johnny Grove, who inspires me and our whole town. In January 2018 Johnny was riding over to help a friend out, it was an icy, early Colorado morning. Before he knew what was happening, his car flipped, ejecting Johnny. He suffered extreme spinal damage. That accident left him paralyzed from the waist down. For all who know Johnny, his paralysis is just FOR NOW. He was a pro-body builder and very active in the soccer community. No one could imagine that such an accident would happen to him.

Johnny is one of my heroes. I see his determination to continue being an amazing dad; he smiles every day because he's genuinely happy. He has the most incredibly positive attitude and spends every spare moment learning how he will walk again. I guarantee, if anyone can do it, it's my best friend. Johnny Grove WILL walk again.

Johnny's life is another example of someone that lives the lessons of this book every day. Daily, he adapts to the effects of this life-altering accident, his grit and determination to walk are powerful. Johnny's Why, is also his family; it drives him to keep going until he achieves all of his goals. He challenges himself every day to grow so that he can once again walk. Johnny strives to be his healthiest because he knows that being healthy will keep him around for years to enjoy his family, and it will be vital to walking. The memories he's creating with family and friends may be different, but they are equally fulfilling as before the accident. He takes nothing for granted and fights for it all each day.

If you still need inspiration, think of Johnny as an example of how there are no excuses.

For more information, check out my podcast, "Matt-Chat" here at www.dadpodneur.com

Final Words

Connect on Facebook
https://www.facebook.com/mattsmithcerealdadpreneur

Or email me your thoughts to
matt@cerealdadpreneur.com

Jenny's Advice

If you just finished reading this book and haven't done everything Matt said, all I can say is, "Why haven't you started yet?

For me, as a spouse, it's easy to support my husband. He's always working to improve himself and our family. I suggest that all the partners out there, ask, "How can I help?"

You and your partner are a team, just like Matt and me. So, work together, come up with a plan, communicate, and continually adapt. Each person has to give 100% for this to work.

About the Author

Selling gum, running paper routes and mowing lawns was the start of Matt Smith's entrepreneurial career. Today Matt is Founder and owner of many businesses including Snooze Mattress Company, the largest Snap Fitness (Pueblo) in the world, Wakeup Marketing and a commercial and residential real estate investor and developer. Matt has started and sold 5 other businesses in completely different industries, and has a genuine love and passion for business and people.

A Pueblo, Colorado native, Matt is engaged with various community organizations. and is a mentor for Fellowship of Christian Athletes. He and wife Jenny have three wonderful children; Parker 6, Paisley 5, and Parker almost 2 years old. Matt's family are his WHY, his driving force. His daily habits and choices revolve around his family and having fun both at home and at work. In his bestselling book Cereal Dad Preneur, Matt shares many lessons and stories to help entrepreneurs balance wealth building, work and family as much as possible. While there is never complete balance, Matt and Jenny ensure that they spend out of school hours

About the Author

together and take many family trips to their mountain home and trips overseas.

Matt can be reached at matt@cerealdadpreneur.com

CEREAL DAD PRENEUR

Open the link below to access your Book Bonus gifts
https://cerealdadpreneur.com/bookbonuses

www.ingramcontent.com/pod-product-compliance
Lightning Source LLC
Chambersburg PA
CBHW052348220526
45465CB00003BA/1008